Sis Selene,

"They only live when it's time to die."
　　　　　　　　　　　　−Umar Bin Hassan, The Last Poets

*"Homicide is the leading cause of death among Black males
ages 15 to 24."*
　　　　　　　　　　　　−U.S. Department of Justice

tough love

THE LIFE AND DEATH OF

tupac shakur

CULTURAL CRITICISM AND FAMILIAL OBSERVATIONS EDITED BY
MICHAEL DATCHER AND KWAME ALEXANDER
with a special epilogue by mutulu shakur

Alexander Publishing Group, Inc.

This text is printed on acid-free paper

PUBLISHED BY ALEXANDER PUBLISHING GROUP
PO Box 21
Alexandria, VA 22313

Book Editor: Jiton Davidson
Cover & Book Design: Toni D. Jones
Photography: Kenneth Nahoum (Courtesy of Death Row Records)

ISBN: 1-888018-05-4
Library of Congress Number: 96-79585

Manufactured in the United States of America
1 3 5 7 9 10 8 6 4 2

To the memory and legacy of
Tupac Amaru Shakur
June 16, 1971 - September 13, 1996

and all the brothers and sisters
whose lives, removed from the earth,
we remember: Rest In Peace!

acknowledgements

Any time you conceive, develop and complete a project of this magnitude in a short period of time (two months to be exact) it becomes a familial effort out of necessity. We have been very fortunate to assemble a talented group of writers who heeded our call for essays, commentary and poetry. Books published in this manner, defying all time constraints, are becoming increasingly prevalent, primarily to capitalize on a very current event (e.g. "The Trial of The Century"). It was our decision to embark upon this journey, not as a commercial exercise, but rather as an act of critical examination balanced with tough love, in an effort to offer political and cultural direction for our community. We are grateful to the following individuals whose timely assistance and cooperation, helped bring this book to fruition: Anita Wall, Hodari Ali, Edwin Avent and USPMG, George Pryce and Death Row Records, Barbara & Dr. E. Curtis Alexander, Pamela Preston, Zenobia Waridi, Dreama Frisk, Marshall Johnson, Faith Price, Lin Woods, Julia Shaw, Sonia Sanchez, Melvin Green, M'lea, Chris Stanley, Rohan Preston, Kerensa Elzy, Meredith Moise, Ultima, Stacy Shelnut, Stacey Evans, Haki Madhubuti & Third World Press (especially Rose), Toni Banks, Fetterrof Colen, Patrick Williams & G2000, Monica Harris, Fiona Williams, Amy Pointer & The UB Graphics Lab, Lamar Redcross, Reverend Herbert Daughtery & The House of the Lord Pentecostal Church, EZ Street, Kalamu ya Salaam, Marvin Hamilton and Natasha Ortiz. Special thanks to Alonzo Brandon, Ivy Stephenson, and Herbert Harmond, for their financial support (Ujamaa!).

We are greatly appreciative to Dr. James E. Savage and Stephanie Stanley of The Institute for Life Enrichment, for their assistance and support of this project. Thanks to Nandi Assata Alexander, a daughter whose love and patience is life-giving and life-saving. We are indebted to two individuals whose unwavering dedication and professional involvement in this project has ensured its success: Our book designer, Toni D. Jones, and editor, Jiton Davidson.

Lastly, we offer our prayers to Afeni, Mutulu, Billy Garland and the family of Tupac Shakur. In the spirit of our ancestors, we say Asante Sana to Tupac for his offering. In Peace.

contents

Preface
Introduction *by Kierna Mayo*

1 DIRECTIONSCORE: NOTES ON A RIDAH

2 VERSES FROM THE UNDERGROUND

3 GATHERING WITNESSES

NOTES

preface

"Each generation must, out of relative obscurity, discover its mission, fulfill it, or betray it."

–Frantz Fanon

Tupac Amaru Shakur was ours. He presented himself to our generation like a gift offering. No ribbons, no bows, no paper. He came in a plain box and he came opened. 'Pac allowed us to peak into the chaos of his life—we saw ourselves. Maybe that is why we embraced him, even when he chose to deny his brilliance in favor of showing his ass. We knew that his screaming THUG LIFE was nothing more than a post-modern, plantation field-holler for help-- an out of key plea for love.

This book is a response to his call. A response that we acknowledge may be late, but not too late. Perhaps, the intense life and death of Tupac, can provide insight and lessons on the purpose and neccesity of dialogue, particularly as it relates to the future of Hip-Hop music. As a generation of "New Jack" intellectuals, our analysis of "Gangsta" rap must move beyond the simplistic review of phat beats and vivid stories of life in the 'hood. This dialogue we speak of must question the overabundance of descriptive lyrics, and challenge the lack of prescriptive lyrics. If we indeed are forward-thinking Black writers/artists, we must choose self-determination over self-destruction; freedom over slavery.

Harold Cruse was correct when he said, in *The Crisis of The Negro Intellectual*, that if black writers don't study and theorize the conditions of their race, white writers will. Hence, when Tupac was assassinated, mainstream media pundits came with the simplistic "Live by the sword/Die by the sword" bullshit analysis that our generation has come to expect from people who are accustomed to dismissing young Black life because they can. They did not speak from a space of love. They spoke as voyeurs, looking into a subculture that they could not feel, that even we sometimes cannot understand. From cultural icon to anti-martyr, Tupac's existence and demise elicits a wide range of opinions, all worthy of commentary. Unfortunately, we cannot rely on the media to offer a holistic view of Tupac, in particular, and Black Culture, in general. We must determine and define the parameters by which our culture, and its stabilizers, are judged. But first we must have serious dialogue. We must speak our own truth. That is why this book is so important.

The writers in this book have attempted to deal with the full humanity of Tupac Shakur. Like many in our generation, he was a man of startling contradictions. 'Pac could call for black revolution in one breath and completely disrespect a woman in the next. He was *freedom fighter* and *counterrevolutionary; African* and *American*. The essays and poems in this work explore the genesis of these actions and link them to the socio-political realities from which they were born. The writers struggle with Tupac as he struggled with himself. Our work is critical but empathetic; passionate about his potential, but clear-eyed in its understanding of where he fell short. We loved Tupac. This is our attempt to tell the truth about his life—and ours.

The Editors

introduction

At this writing, nearly two months have passed since the murder of rapper-actor Tupac Amaru Shakur. On my answering machine is a message from my baby sister who is away at college: *Hi everybody*, her sweet voice dances through the recorder in playback mode. *Kierna, listen, I heard that Tupac got arrested yesterday for staging his own death. Call me.* Beep.

Huh? Well, in reality I'm only slightly puzzled by this bizarre message. It's so silly, I can only crack an even sillier smile. Yet over the past few weeks, lil' sis is hardly the first in our community to suggest that Tupac might in fact still be alive (See Chuck D's online explication: *The 18 reasons why Tupac Shakur is Still Alive*). Listening to the answering machine, I ask myself how is it that so many intelligent black people are having serious discussion about this? Do people really think Tupac Shakur slipped out of Las Vegas' University Medical Center through the back door with one lung? Do they believe he convinced the hospital publicist to go *live*, let alone national, with the lie; the medical examiner to sign the death certificate?

Yet after having reasoned away any possibility of any of the above, and enjoying a quick laugh at the naiveté of my own flesh and blood, something in me still wants to attribute the recent rash of Tupac sightings to truth. I mean, we've been called conspiracy theorists before and damn if the CIA wasn't really running crack through South Central. And, no doubt, from dancing with Digital Underground to transforming into his final alter ego "Makavelli," Pac was indeed a magician, creating and recreating himself right before our very eyes.

But this is deeper, I believe. This unwillingness to let go of Tupac Shakur rest not so much in the tragedy of his sudden death, but in the very significance of his tumultuous life. I raised the topic of my assignment to write an introduction to this collection on Tupac to a group of friends. One brother began to tell me how Tupac was utterly insignificant and never mattered to him. Not in the least bit. Not at all, he said. Of course, he spent the rest of the night talking about the slain rapper.

Since the day Tupac Shakur passed from this life, many black people have rushed to disregard him in an effort to affirm that their politics never had room for his seeming lack of. However, we don't raise the significance of Tupac in death for the purpose of being non-critical of that which was his life. No, instead it is just the opposite.

It is our duty to claim, celebrate and most of all critique the life of Tupac Shakur. Like the black genius Miles Davis, Tupac, too was brilliant. Like Miles, Tupac left a body of work (and even 2 films and 2 albums to be released posthumously) for our consumption. Like Miles (who abused black women), Tupac, too, had vicious demons.

It is important we examine him for the very reason it is important we examine hip-hop. That we recognize the art form for the socio-political barometer it is. Hip-hop is at once a certain painful and glorious truth about where the masses of black youth *really* are today. It is an indictment on america [sic] some 130 years post-slavery, and on the institutions this country still holds so dear-- white supremacy, patriarchy and capitalism. It is our response or lack thereof to these destructive forces.

In a life that lasted a mere 25 years and a career that spanned nine of them, Tupac produced seven rap albums including hip-hop's first double CD. He was known as an impossibly hard worker who would hole himself up in the studio night after night. He won critical recognition in every one of his acting roles. As a testament to his raw talent, in his very first professional part, he peered deep into the possibility of young black insanity and gave us the disturbing, unforgettable character "Bishop."

Tupac was significant. And we know it.

He touched black lives young and old; he was a soul stirrer, and (forgive this) a badboy. White folks, too, had to pay attention to him-- he bucked down their coward cops in the tradition of his mother, stepfather and the revolutionary black nationalist/New Afrikan Independence Movement born in the late sixties.

But shedding light on what was tremendous about him is not to be delusional. Some have foolishly suggested that Pac was our modern day Malcolm X. Not so. Malcolm's life was dedicated to Black self-determination. Be clear, Tupac's life, while it often appeared as though it was autonomous from everything and everyone, was very much controlled. At his worst, he was a threat to black women, other black men and even children.

Tupac's life seemed, almost by design, hand-created for the carnivorous ways of academics, theorists and politicians-- he was after all, a black woman's son. Indeed, they (we) dissect his living and his death like one would a rabbit in Biology 101, half the class deconstructing the creature for greater under-standing, while the other half is satisfied with simply destroying what once was.

As young black writers and lovers of hip-hop, for what it is worth, we are seizing what Tupac's short existence bequeathed us-- before someone else does. In your hand is the first published collection of written work exploring the manchild, Tupac Shakur. By binding together a wide and unpredictable rainbow of black voices, this book dares to be both critical and emotional. The essays, articles and interviews henceforth will alternately make you bitter and hysterical, defeated and hopeful. Tupac the victim. Tupac the villain-- complex, yet so damn simple.

Of course, Pac himself acknowledged he was all these things and more. Certainly, Tupac had a sense about his own being that too few of us have-- like it or not, our lives are what create history. This book, too, is our history; our voices for our children about the best and worst of one of *us*. Read this and further challenge your own ideas on the subject of Pac's micro/macro significance. Depending on how you view it, you too may very well refuse to let him die. As for me, I am convinced the coming and going of Tupac Amaru Shakur boils down to one absolute truth, one historical truth. america [sic] is an impossible place for black people. Sometimes you win, sometimes you lose.

Sometimes you do both.

1
directionscore: notes on a ridah

Tupac's Squandered Gift

by Kenneth Carroll

As rapper Tupac Shakur lay dying in a Las Vegas hospital room, commentators, reporters and critics on the left and right were all easily summing up his tragic life as a casualty of a gangsta rapper attempting to live up to his wrong-headed raps. Their analysis lacked the style or economy of my 14 year old son, who sadly proclaimed Tupac "stupid." My own reaction to his death was to think of the Washington poet DJ Renegade's melancholy libation for the victims of violent crime: "This is for the brothers who found out too late, that going out like a soldier means . . . never coming back."

Shakur's life and death are now in danger of becoming a clichéd object lesson on the dangers of drugs, guns and, unfortunately, hip hop music. But Shakur's dreary end holds another, perhaps more profound, warning about the role of Black artists in an era of crack cocaine. It says clearly that we cannot afford to be minstrels for dollars or our own dreams of stardom. His death was the lamentable loss of a gifted, misguided, young poet who spoke with insight and energy to his hip-hop world, but who committed the unpardonable sin of using his immense poetic talents to degrade and debase the very people who needed his positive words--his fans.

I respectfully acknowledge and dismiss the arguments I know I will get from my outraged literary colleagues when they realize I am calling Shakur a poet. They are probably choking on their herbal teas or cappuccinos. I am a poet whose literary influences include Walt Whitman and Eric B. and Rakim, Shakespeare and Public Enemy, Amiri Baraka and my favorite poet, Henry Dumas, but on songs like "Keep Your Head Up," "Dear Mama" and "Brenda's Got A Baby," one cannot help but be impressed with his use of narrative, imagery and pathos. His storytelling skills, literary craft and his vulnerability shone through on those songs and, combined with his smooth vocal delivery, made him one of rap's most distinguished voices. His songs have nearly become inner-city anthems, and his popularity grew with each album, despite the litany of trouble that accompanied his life. I was not the only writer who recognized Shakur's talents as a hip-hop bard: The great African American poet Nikki Giovanni trumpeted Tupac's poetry and spirit in her recent readings, quoting his lyrics and condemning what she saw as a racist society for trying to silence him.

But as positive, powerful and profound as some of Tupac's songs are, they don't begin to atone for his unforgivable crimes of denigrating women and calling for the murder of other young black men. I do not hold Shakur responsible for anyone who has murdered another human being, nor do I hold him responsible for toxic pollution, the current crisis in the Middle East, welfare reform, or the influx of guns or drugs into Washington or Los Angeles. I do hold him responsible for exploiting the carnage and basking in the mayhem of urban America, where young girls are found raped and killed near their high schools, or where brothers are murdered standing outside their homes playing catch.

In the African American tradition of poets like Baraka and Dumas, we understand that the job of the poet is to celebrate and illuminate. Simply put, the poet is always trying to get to truth and beauty, even as he or she exposes and details the horror that prevents us from arriving at that destination. Tardy apologists and post-mortem Shakur fans are now foolishly suggesting that he and other gangsta rappers were simply exposing America's ugly underside by, as we say in the hood, "keeping it real." This is a grand absurdity posited by music magazine editors who are trying to hype their insipid rags, and by hypocritical radio programmers trying to justify their unjustifiable play lists, which now include a heavy dose of negative rap and generally exclude anything positive or creative.

These apologists must explain how hip-hop pioneers like Grandmaster Melle Mel, Chuck D and KRS-1 managed to "keep it real" without disrespecting their fans or their communities. Amiri Baraka was dragged from his home and beaten by the police; his wife and children were shot at and narrowly escaped death, yet he did not think that calling black women "bitches" would change the direction of the Newark police. Instead Baraka wrote, "Back home the black women are all beautiful... The black women in Newark are fine."

Henry Dumas, a 33-year-old activist-poet, was murdered-- shot in the back by a New York transit cop in 1968, yet his poetic legacy is of beauty and music. When I think of Dumas, I think of his lines, "Bones of my bones/ all you golden black children of the sun/ lift up and read the sky/ written in the tongue of your ancestors." You can also read Baraka's poem "Black Art" or Dumas' "Tis of Thee" and find anger, poetry that is 100 times more fierce and piercing than Tupac's angriest song.

But, like it or not, Shakur was the Baraka or Dumas for a large segment of this generation. To ignore that is to deny his power and miss the chance to influence future rap poets. The danger that gifted hip-hop poets like Shakur pose, is that as grandiloquently as they sing about their mothers or the harrowing conditions of urban America, they are equally seductive in their unbridled exultation of hedonism and death. They will, I guarantee you, have more songs dedicated to their favorite drug than their favorite girl, or they rap more emotionally about their dead homies than their living children. They do not properly illuminate the problems of the society.

In fact, they ultimately obscure its inherent flaws by focusing such rapt attention on themselves. Because Shakur conspired in the rape of a young black woman, and attacked a black movie director on the set, he made it much more difficult for black people to focus on larger realities: Republican attempts to roll back civil rights legislation or the collapse of the inner-city economy or allegations about the CIA and drugs. Gangsta rappers are like brightly colored gnats: They worry and distract more than they menace; they make examining the real problems more difficult.

Unfortunately, many of us who call ourselves fans did not protest loudly enough Shakur's misogyny or violence. This includes Nikki Giovanni, who lauded Shakur as a besieged young African American male without demanding that he stop debasing African American females and celebrating violence. Black women and their children are among the most vulnerable segments of American society, but they could not intelligently look to Tupac's music for respite from apathetic and antagonistic lawmakers. Young black men, whose lives are almost always imperiled, could not turn to Tupac's music to find alternative images of themselves. These were not the people protesting Tupac's poetry, and they should have been.

We cannot depend on folks like Bob Dole or C. Delores Tucker or Bill Bennett, who would have us all listening to their censored Top Ten or the rap version of "Up With People." We, the fans and the members of the hip-hop community, must demand that these poets pit their venom at more appropriate targets and not at those of us who daily strive against deep odds to survive in our communities. We must insist on more radio air play for hip-hop groups like A Tribe Called Quest, Spearhead, De La Soul, The Fugees and others, who use their rap as more than weapons to bash the heads of those who are already getting bashed by a larger bat. We must tell these poets, as Henry Dumas instructed us in his poem "Black Star Line,"

> Sons, my sons...
> Make your heads not idle sails, blown about
> by any icy wind like a torn page from a book

Shakur had some choices, tough choices, the kind you get often as a talented young person in a money-driven society, and he made his choice and had the words tattooed on his stomach: "Thug Life." But we must counsel all hip-hop poets to stand as Baraka and Dumas stood-- with us-- as we stand with them. We must remind them, as we pour libation for the fallen poet Tupac Shakur, that going out like a thug, means never coming back.

MEDITATIONS IN THE HOUR OF MOURNING

by asha bandele

1.

A friend of mine calls, tells me an anthology is being done on the life, impact, and I suppose, the death of Tupac Shakur. Poems, essays, stories, and letters. Says L.A. is in mourning, would I write something? I feel flattered to have been considered. Feel overwhelmed by the request. I mourn the loss of all Black people killed unnecessarily (what killing is necessary?), but my emotions around Tupac are mixed and difficult. I never wanted him dead, used to hope he would change, but what he did while he was alive never impressed me in any positive way.

Still he was the stepson of a man I care about deeply. That's the place where most of my sorrow lies, with the people who loved him since he was a boy, who once saw promise in his 6-year-old eyes, and who pushed and encouraged him to be better, be the best.

I ask my friend, have you contacted Mutulu, what does he have to say? He tells me he's never heard of Mutulu Shakur, and I 'm not surprised. Folks who know about Mutulu, know that he's Afeni's ex, Tupac's step-father, didn't think of him in the hours following 4:03 p.m. on Friday, September 13th, 1996. But it is clear to me that Mutulu, his grief and isolation, should be, and will remain, my first and last thought on Tupac Shakur. It's the thoughts in between I need to work out.

2.

Let me tell you what I remember. I remember girls who were never treated like girls even when they were girls. 12-year-olds and 15-year-olds speeding across childhood fast as night. Tight skirts, big titties and hips dangerously rounded before they were teenagers. It was never a problem getting into clubs, charming drinks out of men old enough to be their fathers. Of course, some of them were their fathers.

Girls lived that way, those who lasted, on a wing and a mother's prayer, slinging, hustling, dancing and dying.

You know what I think? I think everything, all the advertising, all the male-designed clothes, all the characters in movies, on tv, all the music videos, all the child molesters and muthafuckas that don't let you walk down the street without screaming "hey lemme get some, come on bitch, what's yo' number, who the fuck you think you is bitch, you think you too good to speak bitch," all of it tells girls to be whores. And then girls get punished for trying to oblige.

Bitch, ho, freak, nasty girl. That was those girls, but they didn't mean to be. I swear this is the truth. And the truth is always the biggest secret. The truth was each one of those girls just wanted a man to love them, everything they did, was about getting the love they thought they needed. They just didn't know how, and had been taught according to corrupted rules in a corrupted game where no one could ever win. No one ever did win.

I haven't forgotten that this is about Tupac.

But it's also about what I think of most when I think about Tupac. I think about his videos, the girls and the lyrics. And I think about that woman he met on a dance floor. He said she did him between beats, right there, easy. Went back to his hotel and for what? For what they ask? I can't believe they ask. For the secret desires: maybe he really likes me, maybe he'll take me on the road, see the magic in me. I did what he wanted, that's got to mean something, fuck those other women, I'll do whatever he asks.

Just because you can take advantage of somebody, doesn't mean you should, doesn't make you innocent. Does it?

3.

It ain't no fun if my niggaz can't get some. Snoop said that.

4.

Nobody, I swear to God, nobody deserves to have a train pulled on them. You don't come back from that the same, whole. You might look the same, hold down a job, get married, have babies, go to Church, go to court, press charges, but you don't come back from that the same, whole.

5.

And what if it was your daughter? How would you struggle with her if she was out in clubs, tight skirts, grinding, sucking or fucking on the dance floor. Would you call together your friends, tell them, "go ahead, take a piece of her," one after one, leave your stink and spray on her stomach, in her hair, across her face, wrapped around her tongue?

6.

Everybody' s somebody's daughter.

7.

Would we be willing to forgive Tupac if he hadn't been a hip-hop star? If he was just a nigga from the hood? Is sexual abuse okay if you're famous, bad if you're a garbage man?

8.

The first time I met or even heard about Tupac Shakur, it was Black Nation Day, 1992. He did a concert there, a fund-raiser, I think. I was on security, didn't really see the show, and don't remember much about that night except that he showed everybody where he had branded himself right across the stomach, THUG. Oh, and that the crowd of students cheered.

Even still, the nationalists, all of us, young and old, had hope in him. Born in prison to former Panther, stepson of a political prisoner, he was going to be the one, was going to make records about the struggle, carry the torch, take the word to the masses. We really said that.

8.

Ain't nothing but a gangsta party.

9.

Sekou Odinga calls me as I'm writing this piece. Well, it's thought-provoking , he tells me, and we weren't wrong to hope. We're never wrong to hope.

I think about little Dhoruba, the six-year-old son of Nandi and Abdul Majid. Abdul is doing 30 to life in a New York State prison as a result of his Black Panther past. I love his son, miss that boy something terrible when I don't see him, think of him constantly, tell his mama all the time, Nandi, Dhoruba might be the one, the next Malcolm, the doctor to cure AIDS, whatever. I see sun and possibility in that child's eyes. And feel renewed when I look at him. Feel renewed just thinking of him.

No Baba Sekou, we are right to have hope, right to have hoped.

10.

People say Tupac spoke for us.

11.

If Tupac speaks for us, then who do and who did Malcolm X, Ella Baker, Harriet Tubman, Martin Luther King, Sojourner Truth, Cinque, Assata Shakur, Sekou Odinga, Sundiata Acoli, Ramona Africa, Mumia Abu Jamal, George and Jonathan

Jackson and Mutulu Shakur speak for? Do they and Tupac together speak for us? Even if their lives, their words, their actions and beliefs are diametrically opposed, can they really all still speak for us? Is it that we believe that anyone can speak for us as long as they got a good beat, and two or three nice lines in an ocean of blood, of what nigga I'm a kill next, who's bitch I'ma do.

12.
Are we schizophrenic?

13.
Did anyone ever consider the possibility that it was all just about the money? Is that something we can broach? That, *gimme mine, fuck the police* attitude was just part of a big *fuck everybody* attitude? Maulana Karenga posed this question once: who deserves a martyr's immunity against criticism?

   I'm just asking. Was Tupac a martyr?

14.
Why you gotta be so negative. The man is dead.

   My man says this to me one Sunday morning. Other mornings we have criticized Martin Luther King. How did Tupac get exempt?

15.
I think about years I spent slow-dancing with self-destruction. Drugs, alcohol, men, you name it. And all those people, the one's in my family, the one's who became my family, who refused to accept me at the bottom of a well I had thrown myself into. Even mediocrity was rejected because I could be better. And I did get better. And I did do better.

   Criticism?

   I think criticism is a gift we give to people we love. To people with promise.

16.
He was a martyr to the hip-hop nation, girl, have some muthafuckin respect.

17.
Okay I give up, exactly what is the hip hop nation? Where's it located? What's its flag look like? Who are its representatives, its government, its president, its language, its culture, its mores, its laws and symbols?

   What role do the women play there?

18.
Make the revolution and the music will come. Sekou Toure said that.

19.
Frantz Fanon admonished us these three questions:
Who am I?
Am I who I think I am?
Am I all I ought to be?

20.

22 Sept 1996
USP/Florence
Administrative Maximum

Beloved Mutulu,

It's been a week and two days since you lost your son, and all I can do is sit here, pray for you, keep struggling for your release. This is your tenth year in prison, and still people stop me when they see me wearing the T-shirt with your name on it. They say "Mutulu saved my life." I wonder if that can mean something to you now, knowing that even as your son is gone, how many sons are alive as a result of your touch. And daughters too Mutulu, the ones born to you, the one who adopted you, the ones like me, Monifa, and I know there are others.

You know what I heard? I heard when Pac was 10 and they asked him what he was going to be when he grew up he said, "I'm gonna be a revolutionary." Like you, Mutulu. The best and biggest dreams Tupac once held for himself were the biggest and best dreams he saw you accomplish. Never forget that, or that somewhere maybe he's that 10-year old again. Somewhere believing in his own possibility. None of us know for sure, but it doesn't hurt to believe, does it Mutulu?

Nobody should have to lose their child. Nobody should have to suffer that loss as a political prisoner, a person who has dedicated his whole life, since he was a child, to saving children. I just had to say that.

Strange things are going to be said now that Pac is gone. But, those of us not looking for fame in tragedy, will always know that it was you who held him when he was a boy full of tomorrow's promise. Who took him to the store, told him stories of freedom-- showed him, said, "Mama's coming home soon boy, don't you cry." You claimed him even when he didn't claim you. We know that Mutulu, and we honor that, and we grieve with you. We grieve deeply.

And I also have to tell you we will get through this brother, believe me, you are not alone. Even in that prison cell, you are not alone. Can you feel my/our love and prayers? It's a big love, a stubborn love, an undaunted love, I swear Mutulu, an ever-increasing love. It's a love born of your commitment and sincerity, your labor and yes your own love your deep and sacrificing love for Black people. Your love, a manifested thing.

Call me when you can. I'll be waiting, forever if I have to, patient, prepared...

Keeping my head up,
your devoted sister/daughter

asha

Author's Note:
Mutulu Shakur and Sekou Odinga are imprisoned as a result of conspiracy charges arising from the liberation of Assata Shakur.

WALKING THE TIGHT ROPE:
THE ART, REALITY AND IMPACT OF TUPAC SHAKUR

by Bakari Kitwana

The murder of Tupac Shakur is a great tragedy and a waste of a young, promising life. Shakur, at only 25-years old, had come to represent a volatile mixture of youthful energy, exuberance, arrogance, self-confidence and, at times, foolishness. He represented possibility on the one hand and self-destruction on the other. What mustn't be overlooked as the Hip-Hop Community mourns his loss is that there are many young Black men like Tupac Shakur, who although less well-known and less financially secure, are equally caught up in self-destructive lifestyles. Due to a great deal of misinformation and a changing economy, their numbers are growing even as they are being wiped off the planet everyday. Herein lies one of the greatest challenges facing the Black world in the 21st century: how do we combat the dominant public image of young Black men that has largely been produced by mass media? Tupac Shakur's life and death is a microcosm of the larger picture. Do we dare peer into it?

Rap music is no longer simply the local, communal form of entertainment that it was at its inception in the early 1970s. And even the thriving commercial entity it became by the late 1980s—as gangsta rap moved from the margins of hip-hop culture to the center—has already been transformed. Despite the various changes in the rap industry over the last six years, there has been at least one constant: rap artists who have enjoyed international fame and platinum sales due to their ability to shock with Black pathological horror stories and, thereby, entertain. Although some advance it as a musical art form whose artistic, political and social implications have yet to be thoroughly critiqued or completely understood, rap music's firmly entrenched dual role as a corporate business and cultural artform demands that artists primarily project stereotypes of young Black men as reality. Within the music industry the belief persists that images of Black men as gun-toters, drug users, drug sellers, irresponsible fathers, and violent, misogynists are not only authentic representations of Black men, but Black men at their best. And although the rap artform grew out of Black culture, hip-hop culture in the mid-1990s more often mirrors a dog-eat-dog street culture that destroys more lives than it strengthens. As a major rap artist who had an affinity for acting, Tupac often walked the tightrope between the art and the reality.

Like most young people in search of self-definition and focus, thrust into the limelight, Shakur's confusion gained expression in the bad-ass, misogynistic, thug life image he projected as his identity. He carried in his music a certain sense of his imminent violent death by gun violence and urban chaos spun far out of control. As much as he saw young Black men as sacred, he lacked a sense of the sacredness of his own life. The only explanations he offered for the fact that his rebellious persona often carried the message of hatred for his own people (especially Black women) were his popular songs "Keep Ya Head Up" and "Dear Mama." Likewise, he often fell back on his identity as the son of a Black activist as a badge of honor to legitimize him as an authentic member of the Black community—credibility that he still refused to live up to. Failing to resolve these important self-contradictions, he violated many people, including himself. His belief that "only God can judge me" at times set him beyond valuable criticism.

Within the Hip-Hop Community, which far too often fails to be self-critical, Shakur represented something else. In him many saw the range of possibilities for young Black men, many of whom are locked out of the emerging global economy. This changing economy is making possibilities for most more and more difficult. In the face of these narrowing odds, which adversely impact the Black poor, Shakur's message was simple: out of nothing create possibility. Despite the increasing obstacles facing Black youth, he demonstrated that with self-motivation, focus and hard work, one can still exact a tremendous impact on the world. As an actor and rapper this is what Shakur represented. He had a tremendous impact on the Hip-Hop Community, in terms of his own rap style, and in terms of giving critical focus to the reality that lingered in some gangsta rap themes. While some of his lyrics bought into the pathologies, others clarified the economic and racial walls that the Black poor are up against. Neither should be minimized by his supporters or critics. Most certainly, however, it was his love for the so-called underclass, and his ability to use the public space he occupied as a place to voice some of their concerns. This calling survives in his lyrics and endears him to millions of supporters.

In his 1995 Album, *Me Against the World*, Tupac seriously critiqued the state of Black youth culture in the 1990s. After going to prison and surviving the first attempt on his life, he recorded his last album *All Eyez On Me*, which is much more nihilistic than his critical reflection in *Me Against the World*. In *All Eyez On Me*, his attempts to analyze the negativity in street culture is overshadowed by his willingness to glorify it. Despite the cross-section, both efforts are full of the youthful rebelliousness that became Tupac and the Hip-Hop Generation's trademark.

Rap artists like Tupac have long understood that art is a reflection of reality. What rap artists have underestimated is that the images go both ways. Art can and does influence reality. This is particularly true in a video age, in an age of multinational corporations, in a global economy where the dominant images of Black youth are one-dimensional, and are transmitted as entertainment via cable television from economically impoverished, and socially and morally decaying realities; to studios; to video sets; to film; to urban, suburban and rural young minds. On the receiving end, too many folks have not grasped that this is entertainment. And while there are elements of truth within this entertainment, more often what is highlighted are those elements of a subculture which are distortions of Black culture and not Black culture itself. Thus many young people are imitating what they assume to be reality. And while this reality does exist, it is not simply a Black reality; neither is it the dominant reality for Black America. Yet, as we continue to be force-fed this "reality," fewer and fewer of us are able to tell the difference. Events like Miami's "How Can I Be Down" and Atlanta's "Freaknik," which cater to Black youth and where too many of us act out the worst of us, are the painful evidence of what we refuse to acknowledge.

The entertainer who rises from modest means to arrive at great wealth and prominence only to self-destruct is an old tale. Those hawking Tupac T-shirts a week after his death as well as radio call-ins who made outlandish comparisons of Shakur to Malcolm X and blindly advised, "Keep living that Thug Life," may realize this, but their actions only add to the growing confusion. In the final analysis, Tupac Shakur is not the martyr that many will try to make him in death, but a rebel who too often made his moves without a cause. Many who see the beauty and brilliance in hip-hop culture despite its imperfections hoped he would grow beyond this uncertainty, as Ice Cube and others have done before him. They mourn what was and they mourn what could have been. Still Tupac Shakur gave the Hip-Hop Generation much to be proud of, and an equal abundance of stereotypical baggage to carry—which even in the face of his death we are left to bear.

TROUBLED FLIGHT

by *Michael Datcher*

When I was eleven me and my friend Eric were standing side-by-side, in front of our Eastside Long Beach apartment building, tossing rocks in a muddy puddle. We were talking about all the cool stuff we got to see in our building every weekend and sometimes on the weekdays—especially in the summer. That time the police chased Jaime's brother through the complex, caught him in the alley and started beating him upside his head. That time Melvin was on Angel Dust and started taking his clothes off and cursing in the courtyard even though there was no one around. That time a bunch of the older boys jumped on that white girl who lived in the corner apartment and were feeling all over her, and her mother came out with one of those big Chinese swords and chased them away. That time Melvin got stabbed right in front of the building and how that blood was everywhere. Living in our apartment building was like living on a TV show. We laughed. Eric tossed a rock and without looking at me said, "I know I'm not going to live a long time so I want to have as much fun as I can right now." I remember not wanting to turn and look at him because I didn't know what my face looked like. He caught me off guard. I wasn't sure if the loss of my eleven-year-old-cool was evident. Eric was the first boy I heard say out loud what I had thought so many times myself. I tossed a rock. "Yeah, I know what you mean, cuzz. I wanna do everything before I die too."

As an adult, I've shared that conversation with many of my friends. It's unsettling how many of them responded with knowing nods. Young black men begin a flirtation with death long before the kiss. This perverse relationship is most heated in the nation's urban centers where so many of us learned to scowl and hold our dicks long before we could hold a good conversation.

Violence seduces. She lays down, naked, beside us, reaching for our hand, calling our name in a disguised voice that is meant to appeal to our manhood. She whispers, "Don't take no shit." She coos, "Get yo' respect." She moans, "Fuck that nigga." This is why little black boys have to make decisions that little black boys shouldn't have to make. How do I deal with the threat of violence in the neighborhood? Do I walk around scared, afraid of death, terrified to go outside and let people think I'm a punk? Or do I accept the reality of life in the neighborhood, embrace the strong possibility of death and go out and get mine while I can? The preferred choice can be experienced live and direct every Friday, Saturday and Sunday night on the Crenshaw Strips of every black neighborhood. There is a whole generation of young black males who are racing against a clock with no numbers, instead, in their place, the faces of dead homies. A whole generation is racing to get paid, get high, be down, come up, and get over—before they die young. A whole generation squeezed into the passenger seat with Tupac, intoning "I feel you, bruh."

When Tupac Amaru Shakur passed, spontaneous mourning broke out in Los Angeles. Wherever you went, you heard Alpines and Kenwoods thumping *All Eyez on Me*. The album existed as an extended eulogy at the funeral and memorial service that we all had in our cars. 'Pac delivered his own sermon. We were the choir testifying at the appropriate times. The message was especially relevant to the young urban brothers who felt Tupac gave voice to their struggle, a struggle that gets lost in the mainstream media's demonization of the young black male. It is a struggle for manhood amidst pain.

Pain is the operative word here. It's easy to identify black rage in young brothers because it edges from the corners of eyes when you cross us on narrow sidewalks. This pain engenders our rage. Pain with no where to go. No outlet because there is no safe place for young black men to say, "I'm hurting. I need you to love me." In place of these words brothers strike a pose and strike out. This is what Tupac did. A sensitive young man in need of love who had the misfortune of being almost pretty, in an environment where these qualities were not valued. He was a man in pain. When he spat at news cameramen after leaving court during one of his numerous court appearances, he was spitting on the public for not allowing him to exist on his own terms. He was young, black and sensitive in a world that constricted young blackness to being hard, unbending. He was caught up in the ultimate game of twister with a posture that refused to yield to the demands of his rich black humanity.

When he scrawled THUG LIFE across his torso, he was writing a painful treatise on the limited possibilities of his life. A dissertation that he researched by imitating bullshit niggas masquerading as men who learned their ideas about manhood from bullshit niggas before them. THUG LIFE became his mantra. He repeated it each time he made a choice to ignore the brilliance that threatened to make him feel good about himself. Sometimes accepting brilliance can be a hard thing. It can bring a responsibility that can weigh heavy. It brings 25-ton, million dollar questions like, "What now?" and "How can I be brilliant and hard at the same time?"

This is where Tupac got tripped. See, he had the question all wrong. He should have been asking, "How can I be brilliant?"

II.

Tupac had a very problematic relationship with women. He used them. He flattened them out, stacked them up, and climbed them like stairs that led him nowhere. He didn't know that. He thought he was climbing the stairs to manhood. This is a mistake that many young brothers make. Looking for short-cuts up the mountain, when the only true path is the long, spiraling way up and around that mountain. Many sisters witnessed the flattened and stacked course that he was laying but they had love for him anyway.

Tupac was one of the few rap stars who had as many female fans as male fans. Even as he called the first people of the earth "bitches" and "hos," they flocked to purchase his music. Just when they were ready to give up on him, Tupac would find himself and put out a single like, "Keep Your Head Up" or "Dear Mama," and the sisters would forgive themselves again for doubting him. Tupac had a way with the ladies. It was a way, a style, that though often forgiven, had side-effects that were not easily forgotten. The lifestyle of the rapper has forged with the step-brother of the mythical 70's supernigger. The B-Boy poet is swinging in the same realm with Richard Roundtree, kicking down front doors to the 808 bassline of his superhero theme music—with a fine Daisy-Duked sister on his arm. Tupac was right in step. Boasting of sexual conquests like a Caesar's Palace ring announcer. 'Pac wanted it to be known that he got around.

This attitude toward black women is steeped in lucid pimpology. Tupac called sisters bitches then sent them out to make money so they could bring it home to the record store. I have often wondered what goes through the mind of the female rap aficionado who happens to be a fan of a rapper, who refers to her as a female dog.

We hoped for change.

After being charged and convicted of rape, going to prison, and summoning former *VIBE* staff writer, Kevin Powell, to tell the world how much he had been learning about himself, Tupac returned to the recording studio with Death Row being just as hard on sisters as he was before he got locked down. A lot of people hoped 'Pac would emerge from prison a changed man. You know, do the Malcolm thing. Come out talking about nation building and respecting the black woman. It wasn't to be. Death Row was a label that made its name and money on gangsta rap. They used that money to spring Tupac and they expected him to get with the gangsta program—and that's exactly what he did.

'Pac came out throwing up "W's" and screaming, "Westside!" like he was hatched from the earth beneath the corner of Crenshaw and Slauson. He was more Westside than the brothers who were born and raised here. He was a

Westside Rider for life and he took that shit serious. He seemed to want his record company to know how hard he was. That he wasn't no studio gangsta. No Silver Screen gangsta. No bitch-ass nigga. 'Pac was claiming and living Westside like an O.G. to the 25th power. In LA, O.G.'s often treat women like pimps treat their employees.

There were numerous incidents.

Among them, a female fan asked 'Pac for an autograph and received a fist in the face instead. When a black man of Tupac's notoriety treats women the way that he could and did, it sends a very dangerous message: black men don't give a fuck about their women. How can we expect other communities to respect our women if we don't? More importantly, given the great numbers of young female fans that 'Pac drew, what message were they accepting about the role of women in a man's life? Tupac had a lot of juice. Young people especially valued what he had to say. What is the impact on a 12-year-old black girl who knows the words to "Wonder Why They Call You Bitch," like they're lyrics to a Double-Dutch rhyme, or who hears about Tupac socking female fans in the face? What does she learn to accept about the way young brothers will step to her one day? What happens when a young brother, who she cares about, calls her a bitch as if it's a term of endearment? It wasn't Tupac's duty to raise our children or our little sisters, but we're fooling ourselves if we think that his words and actions did not have a significant impact on the way many of his young black female fans viewed themselves.

Amidst all the drama, people often forget that Tupac accomplished what so few of us do—he aggressively pursued his dreams. He dreamed of being an actor. Against the incredible odds inherent in that profession, he made it to the big screen. He was a leading man. At the same time, he dreamed of becoming a rapper and getting his message out to the black masses. Despite limited lyrical skills, he became one of the most popular rappers in the industry. His original message may have been altered by time and circumstance, but it was his message nonetheless. For a young, urban, black man to have the courage to dream, in a world that says there is no room for his dream, is a goal to be applauded. To actually make those dreams manifest is a sign of a very special person. A person to be admired and respected—despite their flaws. Tupac gets love and respect because he was willing to believe in himself, his dream, when no one else would. Although at times, his dream got twisted, he still touched us. He touched the part of us that runs from our own dreams, that caves to our own fears. 'Pac gets love and respect because we all know that to dream is to fly and while we criticized Tupac's troubled flight, we did so safely from the ground.

MAN OF STEEL

by Raoul Dennis

Half the time, it's not about life but instead, death, and what you're gonna do with your time until then. It's not pessimism—just another way of looking at the situation. And there are a whole lot of young Black men who look at it just like that. Tupac Shakur was one of those men.

The majority of people on the planet with something to live for fiend to stay alive and live in fear of motherfuckers who don't care one way or the other about living. Generally, these people know who they are. They have someone or something that makes life worthwhile—so they cling to life. They look forward to each breath, happy about every day they have in this life. And if they really know who they are and truly believe in who they are, they're prepared to die for that worthwhile something if it comes down to that. Now, how many people these days are down like that?

Actually, there are probably sisters and brothers who are more down to die for something than even they may realize. But Tupac Shakur wasn't one of them. He was his own man of steel who had heart but never believed in his soul. The beats were fly, the lyrics were T-U-F-F. He let his nuts hang on the streets and on tracks at all times. But ultimately, he didn't believe in himself or his people. Therefore, he died for nothing. It's not that he left nothing behind. He teamed up with boxer Mike Tyson on a project to support at-risk young people, for example. He died for nothing because for all his influence, the man most of us knew as Tupac Shakur had no plan. And therefore everything he could have impacted, even after his death, went to the grave with him. But there's a few things brothers can learn from Tupac's life and death. Young warriors need to know that it's cool to be hardcore, but stupid to do so without a knowledge of self, a base and a scheme.

By the end of his life, Tupac seemed to want a way out of the gangsta rap game. But he had an image that he created. He was one of the finest lyricists in drawing listeners (whether you were street or not) into a visual understanding of thug life—how and why it existed. He did this so well that he created a stage image that outgrew him. The music artist pretending to be a gangster became consumed by the shadow of the character. Then the artist seemed to become the character and the man became a "gangster." But the gangster wasn't Tupac Shakur's soul. (Remember, this is the brother who began his career with the musical comedy of Digital Underground.) Shakur's soul contained a passionate, angry and sensitive poet who identified with the plight of Black people and addressed it in his music. Anybody who's been shot five times and lived (Shakur's first shooting in New York) can tell you they wouldn't mind a career change. The question is, how do you get out? That depends on the way you got in.

There are several facts known to the Black man's universe that brother Tupac apparently ignored. First, wherever you put your heart and mind, your ass is sure to follow. An intelligent young brother, Tupac still allowed himself to downplay the fact that what he had inside was larger than street life. He saw the big picture that Black people are confronted with. He was almost literal with it: "Until we get free," he wrote "I guess I'll be an outlaw." He even gives props to political prisoners on his last CD. This has to be due, in part, to his family's history of activism. He knew what time it was in America but he chose to put his passions behind thuggin' and sexin'. To an extent, that's cool. As a young man, a brother is entitled to do his fantasy-macho thing. But as a brother with his third eye open, that simplistic, Jesse James ying yang doesn't cut it. Tupac put his mind and heart toward the skin-deep battlezones of the streets. His ass paid the price.

The second undeniable reality is that Black men are not expected to live beyond 25, much less contribute anything. We live with the prospect of death daily. Whether it's the streets, the police, HIV, suicide or just plain stress, most Black men that survive to see 35 whisper a little something to somebody about being glad to have made it. These days, brothers born after 1970 who make it to their 40th birthday will be so happy they're liable to keel over of cardiac arrest at the party. But where was brother Tupac's head in this equation? He had no idea. Tupac Shakur was knocking on death's door as much as any other Black man in America simply because he was here. Although he catalyzed the issue, that's his business. But he could have chosen death—as he did—and still been a badass soldier after leaving this world. He didn't and that's all of our business. Malcolm knew he was marked. King knew. Lumumba knew. So did Medgar and Mandela. As Black men, we all know we're marked. A fortunate man gets to choose when. A fortunate and wise man plans it so that his physical death doesn't end his spiritual life's impact. Shakur missed this, not because he was young, but because he ignored his birthright.

And then there is faith. When brothers had nothing else, there has always been faith. Faith in God, Black women, children—something. Faith keeps one away from the clutches of despair and hopelessness. It instructs that there's a higher order, a brighter day. Tupac knew this as well, but again, he ignored it. His music, ever full of contradictions in spite of the phat rhyme schemes, discussed an awareness of God and spirituality but no commitment to any of it. It's said that you can break a man's body, but until you break his faith, the fight goes on. Without faith, a man is a walking husk with no foundation. Without foundation, nothing can stand for very long.

If brother Tupac understood these things, why didn't he abide by them? If he wanted out of the violence that his image projected, why didn't he walk?

Tupac, like so many passionate and aggressive warriors before him, didn't know how to successfully balance the internal battle between his intellectual, sensitively gifted nature and the social pressure of being a "real man". Huey Newton founder of the Black Panther Party, intelligent strategist and political activist, constantly started fist fights with his own boys to prove he was hard. Malcolm X, who knew of his intellectual gifts at an early age, ran the streets as a hustler, always reconfirming his manhood and status. Many brothers face this dichotomy: brilliance and sensitivity on one hand and sheer self destruction on the other.

Shakur may have wanted to love but he was too far out on a limb to do it and seemingly had no one in his corner to pull him back in. Heavyweight boxer Mike Tyson was fortunate enough to have the Nation of Islam to pull him away from his impending doom and give him a foundation. Not so with Shakur. At the risk of dropping a James Dean cliche, Shakur's only "legitimate" out, as a rebel who forgot his cause, was violent death. For the moneymen of hip hop's hardcore gangsta set, this is the ultimate media-marketing stunt (there are already notions that the murder may have been staged). But there's a power and impact that a man can make even as he sees himself going toward death. The kamikaze pilots of World War II are another example of men who died for something because they saw something in life that made their deaths worthwhile. As much as we can love Tupac for his talents, his humor, his smile and the way he made us relate to his music, he didn't leave us with any meaningful impact—except that he's another dead Black man. The disappointment is that his music could have been a legacy, instead it's just a bathroom bulletin board and he had the skills to do more.

We will love Tupac because he was one of our own, and because if he had been blessed with more time here, we may have been blessed with a forceful visionary and responsible leader once he matured. On the other hand, we fault Tupac because he turned his back on us. He turned his back in that he continued to tell us that thuggin' was the best way he knew. He knew more than that, but he didn't believe in himself or his people strongly enough to commit. So he fell into the very trap that's been laid for us for centuries. And that's too bad because even that punk Superman knew enough to avoid kryptonite.

The Politics Of 'Fuck It' and the Passion to be a Free Black

by Esther Iverem

Grab your Glocks [guns] when you see Tupac.
Call the cops when you see Tupac...
You shot me but ya punks didn't finish.
Now you're about to feel the wrath of a menace.
. . .You know who the REALNESS is

—Tupac Shakur
From Hit "Em Up

If you spent any time at all around Tupac, you saw how easily he let a raised middle finger lead him through the world. Whether he was proclaiming to me in an interview that he stays perpetually strapped and high on marijuana, or spiritedly waving a bottle of malt liquor on the "California Love, Part II" video, his most consistent image was that of a man doing as he pleased, living life by his own rules. 'Fuck it,' the rich young man seemed to say. And if you didn't like it, well then, "fuck you too."

Most of us who have grown up black in America can identify with the quick, bottom-line toughness that sentiment implies. It makes us feel powerful like a Shaquille O'Neal dunk in a society that constantly raises its middle finger to us, or expects us to routinely bend over (Choose your imagery). This feeling of strength is one of the reasons so many people identified with Tupac as a real brother, a sort of 1990's version of what we imagine a free black to be.

But affinity for Tupac mixes what is potentially a positive attitude toward self determination with the worst definitions of that over-used phrase: Keep it Real. At its most meaningful, the phrase urges those in the hip hop nation to remain true to beliefs and rooted in reality. At its worst, it implies that only those things ghettocentric and hard are real in black culture. It endorses the use of street ethics to settle disputes, like the willingness to bust a cap in someone, usually another African-American, if necessary.

Tupac's death is only the most recent and heart-wrenching reminder that with those worst definitions of what is real, we are killing ourselves, carting ourselves off to jail or retiring at a young age to wheelchairs. In many cases, we are denying ourselves an education, love, family or any shot at self or community fulfillment. We are allowing this society to transform us into a self-hating and predatory stance.

Black culture has remade American society's music, style, fashion, all that, says cultural critic and author of "Between God and Gangsta Rap," Michael Eric Dyson. "Because it's been so important, the styles of black popular culture become important to the debates of how we define real black culture.

These debates in popular culture center around who comes from the baddest ghetto, the darkest ghetto. You reduce the complexity, the authenticity of black culture to the ghetto, and reduce the complexity of the ghetto to the gangster."

In the war over who is REAL, (The old man/gangsta rapper Ice-T titles his new album, Return of the Real. A new R&B act calls itself Soul For Real. One of Eazy-E's last hits was Real Muthaphuckkin G's) to the winner, if anyone can win, goes street respect, hood/coast pride and, theoretically, commercial success. Hip-hop was built on a macho foundation of posturing and boasts. Old school acts in New York, such as Boogie Down Productions, Kool Moe Dee and L.L. Cool J. traded nasty barbs over which borough of New York gave birth to rap (The Bronx). Women have gotten into the act too: Roxanne Chante and M.C. Lyte, Queen Latifah and Boss. The level was turned up a few years ago when K.R.S. One grabbed a member of P.M. Dawn off the stage at a show in New York, or when in 1993 Dr. Dre and Eazy-E, and Dr. Dre and Luther Campbell, rapped about and simulated acts of violence against one another on videos.

But the hip hop generation isn't the inventor of this street fuck-it ethos that is violent, reckless or disrespectful of women. The Eastwood/Bronson/Stallone/Schwarzenegger culture that we have grown up on teaches violence as a cause and a cure. Recently, lots of New York rappers seem to be patterning their style after the Italian mob, glamorized in countless popular films such as *The Godfather* and *Goodfellas*. When Shakur made news in 1993 because he was spotted on a Los Angeles-area street, clubbing his Mercedes, it made news while such stupid behavior by drunk frat boys or jocks on a tear is routinely dismissed as "boys will be boys."

We have also been raised to witness a different, masked sort of thuggish behavior on Wall Street, in corporate boardrooms, the Congress or the Supreme Court-- as places that are not the street but that have rendered decisions with the same deadly consequences as Tupac's drive-by shooting.

One of the reasons Tupac [championed] black ghetto authenticity is because it's been marginalized or demonized, Dyson says. The greater energy that the Doles and others in the mainstream spend demonizing black culture, the more [ghetto culture] is about the politics of identity.

The reason the debate is on this level is because we live in a white supremacist society that denies the existence of black life outside the ghetto, he says. For so long now, there's been a narrowing of black culture to a thug or a welfare dweller. What [many rap] artists understand is that you gotta get the foot up off your neck, he adds. The way they go about it doesn't help get it off, but it does draw attention to the fact that the foot is there.

Tupac rapped about the foot on his neck with a lot of swagger and wasn't afraid of crossing the law. One affect is that those who work with young people work to overcome the idea fostered through popular images, such as his, that to be cool or down, you have to adopt an outlaw, fuck-it posture, a lifestyle on the edge. Some black school children trying to be studious are ridiculed by peers who accuse them of trying to act white, as if millions of blacks with academic achievements are not REAL blacks.

The media glamorizes a laziness, the minority in our community who do not want to work, who enjoy substance abuse, says wadud [sic], a 27-year-old, Philadelphia-based recording artist and teacher. "You have young people who aren't reading anyway, who are constantly being told to turn on the TV. On the video, there is someone who looks like them holding a blunt or a bottle of alcohol, sitting with women with no clothes on, making a lot of money. He becomes a hero. He looks like them.

What is the image of a smart black person? he asks. Who wants to be like Urkel? (the black nerd from the ABC show Family Matters). The state of fun-ness is acceptable, and reading and learning are wrong."

wadud works in Philadelphia's high schools and juvenile prisons. He spends days teaching a 16-year-old his ABC's, drilling a 17-year-old in how to spell *sat, pat, bat*. "Is he going to become a doctor? a lawyer? a teacher? a plumber?" wadud asks, then puts himself in the place of his young students: "My time is spent in stressful relaxation. I can only have a conversation about sports and television. I don't know what affirmative action is...I can only hook up with sisters who can only talk about hair and fingernails and boys. Whether you realize it or not, that is a very stressful life. What is the escape? The escape is what they see on the television, the blunts, the forties...just chillin'."

Carlotta Miles, a Washington, D.C. child psychiatrist and psychoanalyst, works with young people in independent schools who generally have more options. In this group, she says, there are also pressures to be real and down in ways that can be self-destructive.

"So our children are imaging themselves not after us," she says. "Successful people are bashed. I think that we need to get out to young people that everything and everybody is not OK. A Teen-age boy who treats young women badly is not OK. A young woman who dresses in a way to expose parts that should be under wraps in not OK. A child who disrespects his parents is not O.K."

The expectations and demands of being real are cyclical, rather than one way. Fans of artists make their own demands for authenticity. When rap artists have been perceived as being too mainstream with no street credentials, they have been dissed like M.C. Hammer and The Fresh Prince).

"As an artist, you have to prove that you are keeping it real," says Havelock Nelson, rap editor at Billboard Magazine. "You're between the mainstream world, corporate people and TV stars, and people in the community. You want to enjoy the fruits of your success, the nice house and car, but at the same time be able to smoke a blunt on the corner with the boys."

Nelson points out that being down isn't about being broke. The lavish lifestyles depicted in rap videos shot at rented mansions send the message that all that can be had by really doing nothing or having fun. But in real life, if you're not rich, the only way to get money by not working is mainly through illegal means.

"Everybody wants to be 'Big Willy' now," Nelson adds, using the current term to describe a big boss, someone large and in charge with lots of cash. "The Big Willies in Harlem are the guys hustling and pimps. Kids don't see the entrepreneurs. Whenever you go to speak to a group of school kids about your job, they say, 'that's cool, but how much money do you make?' That's the first question that people want to ask you. You try to explain that there are certain steps that you have to take to get in school to get to the top; take an internship, maybe work for nothing. But they don't want to hear that. They want it NOW.

"The message sent by a lot of rap artists is "You're the man. Do what you want," Nelson says. I've seen artists light up a blunt in a restaurant. Tupac gets in trouble over and over again. People say, 'you got shot and survived.' And then he says, 'Yeah I'm bad. I'll keep doing it!' But for everything there is an endgame."

While 1960's revolutionaries have taught us about being willing to die for what we believe, it is totally a different matter to die in gang violence or over a high stakes game of Yo Mama, proving your realness by how much you can bluff, how many bullets you can take, how many times you can cheat death.

Afeni's Baby

At first glance, Tupac would seem an unlikely candidate to emerge as a premiere media symbol of the ghetto gangsta-as-authentic black, or the young man saying 'fuck it' appearing with near-naked black women in his videos, referring to them as ho's and advocating violence against other black people. His mother, Afeni Shakur, was a black panther and he was exposed to some of the politics of community betterment through individual and group struggle. But though he respected his mother's teachings, he was also disillusioned by his mother's addiction to crack in recent years and what he called the futility of political struggle. He didn't know if what the Black Panthers accomplished amounted to very much.

He was a study in extremes. He was a small, wiry man, not nearly as big as he looked on film and video. He had a look of hardness from his chiseled cheeks and thick eyebrows. But his sensitivity still shined through his big eyes and long eyelashes. The sensitive Tupac is the one who rapped the social anthems, "Keep Ya Head Up" and "Dear Mama," the one who starred as a sensitive postal worker in the film *Poetic Justice*. The thug fuck-it Tupac is the one who appeared in the movie *Juice*, in which he played Bishop, a crazed young man who winds up shooting his friends. Some people think that with all his posturing, Tupac was just playing a role, playing Bishop. But on the other hand, maybe when he played Bishop, he was just playing himself.

He began his rap career with Digital Underground in 1991, and followed that with two solo albums that expressed his hatred for the police and championed the cause of young black men by basically advocating a law-lessness that he eventually referred to as 'Thug Life'-- a phrase tattooed on his belly. He told me that his Thug Life movement was "for all the underdogs, all the niggas with no daddies...all the niggas in juvenile hall in jail and everything." But his movement had nothing to offer his would-be followers except for an eventual ticket to jail. Before he was sent to prison, he had been accused of a variety of infractions, including assaulting a limousine driver, assaulting director Allen Hughes after being fired from the film *Menace II Society* and an arrest for carrying a concealed weapon.

He was black America's James Dean for the '90's, young, brash, beckoning trouble. His aura as black bad boy was only enhanced when he survived being shot five times during a robbery outside a Manhattan recording studio in 1994. Shortly after, he was convicted of sexual abuse and served 11 months in an upstate New York prison before being bailed out by Marion Suge Knight, CEO of Death Row Records, who immediately signed him. While in prison, his album, *Me Against The World* went to number one on the charts and sold 1.8 million copies. After his release, a hastily made 2-CD album, *All Eyez On Me*, sold 2.8 million copies in less than a year, while *the don killuminati*, an album released posthumously, sold more than a half million units the first week of its release, according to SoundScan.

Tupac made the last moves in his career under the wing of Knight. Knight, himself has been charged with weapons offenses and has been accused of using strong-arm tactics to get up-and-coming artists to sign with his label. Affiliated with the Bloods gang since his youth in Compton, Knight has been known to wear a large diamond and ruby ring that reads M.O.B. and decorated his office in red, the color of the gang. The logo for Death Row Records is a man strapped to an electric chair with a sack over his head. Knight told VIBE Magazine that he chose the name and emblem for the company because most everybody has been involved with the law, for example, Snoop Doggy Dogg, who has also sold millions of records. Dr. Dre, Death Row's major producer/talent, recently left the company, saying to reporters that the environment was too negative and that he's really not a gangster.

Death Row has also been the key player in an alleged East Coast-West Coast war of words, posturing and, some say, violence between Death Row and New York's Bad Boy Records, which includes The Notorious B.I.G., Junior M.A.F.I.A. and Faith Evans on its roster.

Tupac's rage and nihilism helped to kill him. He sometimes sounded crazy, threatening and dissing his perceived East Coast enemies and claiming the toughness-as-realness mantle for his own. In "Hit 'Em Up," the B-side offering on the hit single "How Do You Want It," he warns:

> My 4-4 (.44 caliber weapon) makes sure
> all your kids don't grow...
> You can't be us or see us.
> We're Westside 'til we die . . .
> We do our job!
> You think you the mob?
> We the motherfuckin mob!
> Ain't nothin' but killas in the REAL niggas.
> All you motherfuckers is fillers.

War is Real

There is a war on for our hearts, minds and bodies. On the one side there is a cardboard, short-thrill, fast-kill realness that easily says fuck it. On the other side, there is another notion of realness that includes love and respect for self and others, and a commitment to community betterment. If we and every African-American born after us believe that "aint nothin' but killas in the REAL niggas," then we're going to lose this war. We'll all wind up like Tupac.

There is this inescapable fact about nihilism. You may easily say fuck it to the world. But all that means is, sooner or later you'll wind up fucked yourself.

CROSSROADS TRAVELER

by Angelo Antwone Williams

The Dedication
To the Riders: The natural born hustlers of Leimert Park and the entire Black world
To the Spirits: My grandfather Walter Williams, Tupac Shakur and Robert Johnson
To the future: My sister Angelique and her children: Luca, Jesse and Judah

The Invocation
The world spins around us
We search for a balance
The secrets lie in darkness and light

> –Gil Scot Heron, "Spirits" from the album *Spirits*

Events take on a second life when memory and wisdom mingle to give purpose to the past.

> –Michael Eric Dyson, "The Lives of Black Men"
> *Between God and Gangsta Rap*

Tupac Shakur may well be the reincarnation of Robert Johnson.

We who remember Robert Leroy Johnson, know of his fast rising star in the south and the Blues he banged out by guitar better than anyone else. At twenty-seven, Johnson was the master, a crown given by his peers, the blues men of old-- Son House, Ike Zimmerman, Sonny Boy Williamson (a.k.a. Little Boy Blue), Robert Nighthawk, Howlin' Wolf. But just as his star began to shine he was taken by strychnine in his whiskey, the plot of a jealous husband whose wife Robert was sweet on. To the Blues world, to the Black world his death came shockingly, suddenly. The aftermath of his life was quickly clouded in shrouds of secrecy and mystery. Legends tell of Bob's "deal with the devil" that finally had to be paid off at the crossroads.

We who remember Tupac Amaru Shakur, bore witnesses to his supernovic ride to stardom and record sales. We watched him rise and reflect us in his triumphs and tragedies-- when he conquered and contradicted. We felt and fought for him after his Times Square ambush and questioned his actions or lack there of in the assault of a sister sodomized. We spoke with him when he sang "Me Against The World" and we watched with anticipation for the future when he beckoned us to place "all eyes on him." We shed salt water tears on September

13th as his passing left hollows in our hearts. The Rap world and the Black world mourned. Adolescents mourned a martyred member of the unified young self, the old mourned his potential to be that which never was. Questions quickly surrounded his death and a "who did it" list spawned sporadically spanning from the FBI, to Death Row President Marion "Suge" Knight, to crazed Bruce Seldon fans, to *Source* Magazine for fanning the flames of a wax-born East vs. West Coast rivalry.

Tupac continuously spoke of choices. He bade us to make the right ones while continuously making the wrong ones for himself. Tupac spoke of death around corners, dying tonight, tears, temptations, and his mama-- our mothers (on and off welfare). He spoke of his ambitions as a rider, as a revolutionary searching and ending up at the intersection of Koval and Flamingo at his cross-roads, our intersection.

Robert Leroy Johnson (RL) in 1938 and Tupac Amaru Shakur (Pac) in 1996 have left us at the same place-- searching. Within this same probing space two men shared a search for their fathers, similar social situations in their youth and adolescents, a penchant for traveling, a musical tradition and like lyrics, similar physical features, a love for women, ruling orishas [See Author's Note] cross-road omens and the ruling deity of both men. Along the African American community crossroads, these two men, the conditions surrounding their lives and death stand closer than the sixty years that separate them. In the middle of this road, the similarities between the life, music, and death of both men are at best, a crucible we should all comprehend and heed.

Nay sayers will surely protest putting such importance on what has been reported in the media as another nigga death-- a death deserved. Still others may not allow themselves to believe in reincarnation because of a strong Christian background. But even the most devout Black Christian knows that superstition has some merit; that salt over the shoulder wards off evil; that brooms should never sweep the feet of the living. We know that no matter how straight laced we come to church, the spirit will catch us and move us in ways that wade us in the waters of Africa. Yet regardless of our New World doubts, we can agree on the fact that Tupac Amaru Shakur had Robert Johnson's hell hound on his trail since birth.

I got to keep movin'
I've got to keep movin'
blues fallin' down like hail
blues fallin' down like hail

Umm mmm mmm mmm
blues fallin' down like hail
blues fallin' down like hail
And the days keep on worryin' me
there's a hell hound on my trail
hell hound on my trail

          –Robert Johnson, "Hell Hound on My Trail", *The Complete Recordings*

On Fathers

Tupac, the traveler, began his current ride sometime in late 1971 at the moment of conception. Here at the beginning of his travels a life long search is first unfolded. The question of his father's identity would send him from city to state crossing coasts to finally settle, temporarily, under the wing of another fatherless child. Tupac was to search for his father his whole life and when he found Billy Garland, his biological father (actually Billy found him in a New York City Hospital), Tupac's adolescent years had already passed, as the opportunity for the guidance that he needed to grow into manhood had also passed.

RL was never to know his father either. Ed OG's 1993 rap release, "Be a father to your child" could have been applicable in 1911 in Hazelhurst, Mississippi where Robert Leroy Johnson was born. On May 8th of that year, Johnson began his search for his father but was never to find him. Both men were estranged from their fathers and were dramatically affected by the lack of paternal guidance.

So too are we as a community in search of fathers. Not only are we looking for men missing in action, we are looking for guidance, a unified direction. Our cultural crisis continued as we watched Tupac gunned down. Tupac represented the sum total of our efforts in America for equality from 1971 to 1996. He turned out just as confused and contradictory as our means in making social justice. Tupac died in a hail of bullets that pierced the mountainous "white man is wrong" rhetoric with hollow tips of an incident which may turn out to be simply some "niggah shit." When we do not nurture our own culture and the potential prophets that we produce, how do we expect to get out of the desert, how can we cross over Jordan? The coming generations of fatherless children growing into prime-time thugs could be the final toll paid for the lack of guidance by black men. But the definition of a *thug niggah*, though enhanced greatly by the lack of paternal guidance, is founded upon a lethal dose of scandalous social conditions.

On a Thug Life

The past quarter century is summed up within Tupac Shakur's life-- thug life "The hell you give little children," Shakur said in one of his many *VIBE* interviews, "fucks everyone...That's what Thug Life means."

In February of 1971, Tupac survived his first prison term from within his mothers womb while she was incarcerated on charges of conspiracy to bomb New York public areas. On lockdown since birth, Pac's tour of duty at The Women's House of Detention was followed by successive trips to jail from Oakland to Rikers and further stood as an archetype for an entrapment of ideas, of aspirations, of hopes, of dreams...deferred.

By the time Tupac came into this world on June 16, 1971, the "shining serpent thankful to god" (the literal translation of his name) was road weary, having run the streets with a young Black Panther. Afeni, who joined the Party at 22, had proven herself a solider-incarcerated-martyr-mother in the three years before she brought the product of her loins and goings into being. And so twenty-five years ago a child was born, a son was given into perpetual motion and in search of self. Money and the lack there of was one of the factors that made his mother move from the Bronx to Harlem to Baltimore to Marin City to Oakland to Michigan. But of all his stops the one that Tupac says saved him was to the Baltimore School for the Arts where he first acted in Lorraine Hansberry's *A Raisin in the Sun*. In Baltimore he began writing rhymes, a trade that eventually got him out of the ghetto but unfortunately, not out of the hell that lay before him. His time on stage was cut short when he was moved again to California.

Robert Johnson felt the hell given to little children in a post-emancipation America. Johnson and his family suffered under uneven social conditions as sharecroppers. No longer under the physical lash, the turn of the century Africans in America bore the brunt of an economic determinism that saw them as perpetually dependent and poor. A self described "down home boy," R.L. was reluctant to get behind the mule, till the earth and pick cotton because of the brutality of the work and the wages that were a perpetual trap. Johnson jook-jointed all around the South and the North and made twenty-nine recordings for a division of the record industry that would be called "race records." Robert Johnson, as most of our people, saw his way out through music. As entertainers or simple spiritual singers, our music is, as Art Blakey put it, "the stuff that dusts off the dirt of life."

On Race Records and Gangsta Rap: The Blues Then and Now

Race records could be described as the then modern day gangsta rap. Named after the "race men" of the early twenties, race records were a specialty genre of the recording industry that catered specifically to black people. White record executives came up with the idea to sell blues to black people, and not only did black people buy their own music, other communities followed suit. As race records grew in popularity record executives became ashamed of such a blatant title and tried to change it to a more respective title either "ebony" or "sepia" records and after 1949 transformed a once hush-hush industry into the modern day category of Rhythm and Blues.

Gangsta rap was the same. A specific genre of music was created and exploited by record executives who wanted to sell more records. The high violence and drug escapades depicted in the lyrics, began as a description of the changes in the black community during the 1980s.

It is strange that Tupac's death, in part due to his gangsta image, comes at the same time that accusations surrounding the 16 year crack war on the Los Angeles Black community surfaces. Crack and Tupac matured simultaneously. Since the late 1970's, crack cocaine has made its home in the black community via Freeway Rick Ross, Daniel Blandon and their friends at the CIA. John Singleton said it well in his 1990 movie *Boyz In The Hood*. Talking with Tre, the young brother that makes it out of the ghetto and to college, Ice Cube's character, Doughboy, proclaimed that "either they don't know, or they don't show what's happening in the hood."

As a member of NWA, Cube wrote his lyrics like anthems and his anthems read like headlines: *Street Stories Of The Effects Of The Crack Trade On The Black Community*. L.A. street stories got glamorized when exported to St. Louis, to Texas, to Cincinnati and the simulcast became exaggerated to ballooned states of reality and realness. Along with crack, these hyperbolized stories warped their way into rap, re-creating Pacific Coast Players in absurd places like Paris...Texas. Once fertile and fermented in young minds of the Midwest, niggafied nightmares went rancid creating grotesquely-capped caricatures of little ashy-kneed black boys from L.A. Reality turned to invention and innovation took over when the gangsta image sold records quicker than positive rap.

The gangsta image took hold and record executives from Interscope to Geffen demanded little black gangsta sambos to sell. With the demise of Shakur many in the industry have proclaimed the end of gangsta rap. The pressure for this may be coming from black consumers who have had enough of the hyperbolic side of a real issue. "Keep it real" is the new epithet and so record companies may follow suit again producing the *realest* of the real MC's for sale. But we must remember that the majority of connoisseurs of gangsta rap are not people of black culture but an audience that thrives on the thrill-kill cult of black-on-black violence and a hardness lacking in their own lives. Needless to say, race records and gangsta rap are the genres that both Johnson and Shakur were placed into and it is in these two genres where the two musicians' songs and the two men's travelin' lives display some similarities of note.

Travelin' Men, Music and Elegba

Robert Johnson became a stone traveler. He developed a penchant for it. Awake or asleep, anytime of the day or night, he was ready to go anywhere, even back the way he had just come. Traveling was the main thing...
    -- From the liner notes of *The Complete Recordings of Robert Johnson*

From his birth home in Hazelhurst, Mississippi to as far north as Canada, and all points in between, and finally to his last destination in Greenwood, Mississippi and death, Robert Johnson was a man on the move.

From birth in the Bronx to life in Harlem to Baltimore to Marin City to Oakland to Michigan, to Los Angeles to Atlanta to Times Square to Rikers Island to Hollywood to New York and finally to death in Las Vegas, Tupac Shakur was a man on the move.

Both men were on the move, but where were they going?

Tupac's last two albums seem obsessed with traveling. Tupac was moving around in most of his songs, if not by title he traveled from place to place in content. "Death Around the Corner," "Picture me Rollin'," "My Ambitionz az a Ridah," are some of the more blatant examples of movement. A comparison of two similar songs in the repertoire of both men speaks to this movement. Notice that both men are haunted by a specter giving chase and both have a second sight into a world that most of us refuse to see. Tupac's "Death Around the Corner" seems to be the more morbid of the two, but remember that hell hounds are the keepers of the gates to Hell. When fully understood, RL's vision mirrors the grotesque sight of Shakur's traveling terror, a stalking by something unidentifiable known as Death:

I got to keep movin'
I've got to keep movin'
blues fallin' down like hail

blues fallin' down like hail
Umm mmm mmm mmm
blues fallin' down like hail
blues fallin' down like hail
And the days keep on worryin' me
there's a hell hound on my trail
hell hound on my trail
If today was Christmas eve
and tomorrow was Christmas day
Aw, wouldn't we have a time baby
All I would need my little sweet rider just
to pass the time away, huh huh
to pass the time away
You sprinkled hot foot powder, mmm
mmm, around my door
all around my door
You sprinkled hot foot powder all around
your daddy's door, hmmm, hmmm, hmm
It keep me with ramblin' mind rider
every old place I go
every old place I go
I can tell the wind is risin'
the leaves trembling on the tree
hmm hmm hmm hmm
All I needs my sweet woman
And to keep my company, hey, hey, hey,
my company
    —Robert Johnson, "Hell hound on my trail," *The Complete Recordings*

I see death around the corner
Gotta stay high while I survive
In the city where the skinny niggahs die
If they bury, bury me a G' niggah
No need to worry I expect retaliation in a hurry and I see
Death around the corner

Whisper: What you see?
            What you see?

I see death around the corner

Any day tryin' to keep it together no one lives forever anyway
Stugglin' strivin' my destiny's to die, finger on my trigger no mercy in my eyes
In a ball of confusion I'm thinking about my daddy
mad than a mutha fucka they never should have had me
I guess I seen too many murders
doctor can't help me so I'm stressing with my pistol in the sheets
it ain't healthy
Am I paranoid?
Tell the truth
I'm out the window with my AK ready to shoot
Kill my damn self but I see
Death around the corner

–Tupac Shakur, "Death Around the Corner," *Me Against the World*

   Johnson's hell hound helped him to see the dogs of Hades behind him, while Tupac's hell hounds helped him to see death around the corner. Elegba, the leading orisha of both men, welcomed both men to make a move, left or right, in a world where truth and falsehood are seldom black or white. Like a magician sawing a self in half, the destructive and constructive parts of a person can rarely be clearly severed from one another. Our "down home" Christian values tell us that God is on high and the devil down low. Whereas our "back home" African orishas say that we are a complex mixture. Truth, lies, right, wrong, God and the devil are more often than not intermingled parts of the same whole. When we seek to sever one from the other we usually end up in the midst of a contradiction that immobilizes us as a headless torso in travel, a divided self, a double consciousness. Tupac experienced his "ever twoness" as he tried to explain the contradictions of severing ties with thug life in jail and re-igniting its brutality on Death Row [Records] upon his return to society. 2Pac was never to be one way, he was always going to be a dual self. In a world that cannot negotiate this twinned self, we are seen as schizophrenic, pathogenic. Traveling to the beat of another's drum often finds us a menace to the society we are trying to be in line with. Until we can negotiate the space of our existence to accommodate our reality, some of us will always seem dysfunctional.
   Robert Johnson's hell hounds are the dogs of Hades, the workers of the trickster that obscure clear sight and make it hard for us to balance ourselves

and our lives. They are the paranoia that follow all Africans in America, the fears that keep us crossing over Jordan when it is obvious that we should have gotten there by now.

The question at our community crossroads now is how we see ourselves in our own culture and what parts of our Diaspora can we pull upon to service us in defining our role personally and culturally in a world that is most definitely ours but is more often than not defined on another culture's terms. The way we look at life and death, choice and predestination are important. We can glean a more balanced path of life and our choice from the way of Ifa, an 8,000 year old philosophy that originated with the Yoruba peoples of Nigeria, West Africa. Of Elegba/Esu, one of the main orishas of Ifa, it is said that he "represents choices--your choices." That you see them as limited is simply your perception. Esu/Elegba, unlike the Christian notion of the Devil, does not tempt you or encourage you to make the wrong choices.... When you of your own volition, choose the wrong course of action, he uses these same actions to punish and point out your foolishness. Cruel? No, simply real. If we cut down the trees of the ancient forests, pollute our waters and poison our air, the results will be as harsh and definitive as any that Esu could conceive. Neither he nor the universe, in which we are a part of, "forgives." If we survive our mistakes we learn from them. If we sacrifice, we prosper and survive. The question of community self-definition and determination then are at the cornerstone of this diasporic lesson. After this crossroads, after this crucible, we must come to terms with the definition and in defense of what our community is, and is not.

On Commerce vs. Culture

Historically, since African Americans were purchased, stolen and sold from Africa to the Americas, we were entered into a relationship of slave to master, product to consumer, commerce to connoisseur. Evidence of this continuing relationship is seen in the white teenage mass who purchase the mainstay of rap music. The thrill of the kill and the reality of the streetlife draws billions of other people along with their cultures to supposedly view what is real. Surely the thrill seekers would be shocked to hear that Tupac took ballet lessons in Baltimore. But the market does not want to hear about humanity, they want, we want, items easily digestible, one-dimensional gangstas and thugs that go down easy with milk and cookies at the commercial break. But we have yet to dissect ourselves and our culture from commerce. To the extent that our culture remains on the market is the extent that we will remain enslaved to myopic visions of who we are as a people, culturally and personally.

As if a first born Jewish boy in Herod's Egypt, this little black boy was born with a price on his head. Marked as an endangered species, Tupac turned a seemingly indelible toe tag into a multi-million dollar entertainment career. "It's only music," Tupac proclaimed on his 1994 release *Me Against the World*. As we mourn the loss of another "shinning black prince," I only wish Tupac's words were true.

Clint Eastwood seems to live in the world Tupac wished for. A world were Eastwood, playing the part of Dirty Harry, can buck down the bad guys (*read: busta*) with his .44 and still make it home in time to successfully run for mayor of Malibu. Tupac did not live in that world. The world where human beings can be separated from the killers and thieves they play. Anthony Hopkins lives in that world. No one ever asks him if he still eats human flesh nor do they mistake him for Hannibal Lector.

Part of what fueled the flame of Tupac's quintuple platinum record sales was his cold-hard-crazy image. His constructed stature like coal burned well in a society and an industry that favors hyperbole and heroics. Particularly on his last album, Tupac was aware of his image and the great potential to sell a tattooed, leather clad, oversexed, indestructible, object. In reality Tupac was much less hard of a person and much more a person hardened by adversity. Shakur's deal with the devil may have been no more than a conversation with himself. A simple justification displayed in a paraphrase of one of his many post-penitentiary quotes, "I can't get out of the game, so I'll be the ultimate gamer, the mercurial Machiavelli, that boss player, who takes this rap s---- to the next level." The difference between *All Eyez on Me* and Tupac's previous releases (*2Pacalypse Now, Strictly for My Niggaz,* and *Me Against the World*) is how the content of his songs creates a character and unreal persona that is not human in a three dimensional way but is simply a summation of contents of those songs. "Let us make man," Tupac seemingly says when he speaks of his player image. But this man is not human, he is the ultimate icon of steel and substance that is assimilatable in a world that yearns for celluloid objects. In his first three releases he is a black revolutionary, teaming with the likes of Ice Cube to preach a sermon strictly for his own people. Thug life meant the life that we were given, and the hell that it produced in little children. He asked our mothers on welfare to keep their heads up. He spoke against police brutality and called for the death of crooked cops. With the ladies he definitely got around on the underground but he let them know he was a player.

The trials of getting arrested for J-Walking in Oakland, charged with rape in a crime he may have had no part in, after being ambushed in Times Square-nearly loosing his life and genitalia, Tupac emerged with a few things to prove.

First he had to establish his manhood and so the woman he married while in jail was the first causality of a man who had to prove that although he lost one, he still had it. Thug life on *All Eyez on Me* is still the life he was given, but it warped itself from a social commentary into a drink; Thug Passion, two parts Alize, one part Cristal. He still wanted to tell the ladies to keep their heads up but he was busy watching his back for the bitches. As defined, bitches being women out for his money, and to bring a brother shame. He still spoke against police brutality but focused more on exacting revenge on other black men who either knew the assailants in his ambush or were the assailants. He picked Biggie [Rapper, Notorious BIG] and Puffy [Bad Boy Entertainment President, Sean "Puffy" Combs] more likely than not because he knew that they knew who hurt him and didn't tip him off, not because he thought they did it.

On Summing the Similarities in Men

Johnson and Shakurs lives and deaths seem to exist in parallel worlds. Though they were 60 years apart their lives were both fast, brutal, compact, and celebrated. They shared similar life situations, a thug life whether sharecropping or hustling. Their music strikes a cord in a 400 year-old sorrow song that is African-American, that plaintive wail that is the blues, that is rap, that is *us*. Shakur and Johnson died at the hands of others in issues concerning someone other, than themselves. A jealous husband did Johnson in with strychnine, a rival of Suge night may have pulled the trigger that ended Tupac's life. The theme of their lives was "the crossroads," choices made by, and for them. They kept traveling in a litany of morose movings towards quick death and an avalanche of after-death analysis. Sixty years separate, Johnson and Shakur were born a month apart and died a month apart. May 11, 1911 brought Johnson into being and June 16, 1971 gave the world Shakur. Both men died in their mid-twenties; Tupac at 25 on September 13, 1996, Robert Johnson at 26 on August 16, 1938.

I remember Tupac Shakur. Much in the same way that my grandfather favored the 1930's blues star, I continue to see fragments of my self in Shakur. I have seen his crossroads, and continue to open my eyes to Elegba every morning.

"Heaven for THUG niggahs?" Tupac has answered that query for himself now, but what of us earthbound travelers. We may ask ourselves where is he now and will continue to never know. One thing is for sure, we know where he has been. His shoes trod the same dirt and asphalt as ours, that is if we choose to check out the bottom of our feet. That is if we choose to confront the contradictions within ourselves that Shakur was quick to pick out in himself. Our personal signpost ahead asks us to question ourselves concerning our personal contradictions that supersede religious tenets. There are basic laws of self and community that we as a people need to practice. There are some laws of self preservation that we need to revisit. We also need to revisit questions of cultural ethos as well as religion. We need to revisit Africa at work in our orishas. We need to look at voodoo, scary though it may seem, as the only religion that posed a physical threat to Western European Imperial carnage. The Haitian revolution was led by Toussaint L'Oveture, but the deity that brought them into war was the deity, Oshun. We need to look deep into ourselves as we are positioned in the West and how we got here. We need to make a symbolic and literal retracing of steps of our migration West; Back through Texas, back through Louisiana, back through North Carolina, back to the seasoning and slave markets in Haiti, back to Elmina, back to the land of blacks. Once we have the map of our travels we can easily ask ourselves where we are and who we are and what we will do, and what we won't do.

One of the biggest signposts up ahead of us as African Americans reads Culture vs. Commerce. This query we must answer. W.E.B. DuBois asked us almost a 100 years ago to question our relation to capitalism based on the history of being human capital; real estate. For all of us who consider ourselves hustlers in the game, we must begin to ask ourselves whose game are we playing? De La Soul so accurately described and opposed our super materialism in their recent single The Stakes is High from the same titled album. They queried our monikers of success and questioned our moneyed motives. We must know that freedom's cost is not affixed to the price tag of a pair of Versace glasses. The cost of true freedom is sacrifice.

To speak of Tupac Amaru Shakur is to speak of sacrifice. It is to speak of a little boy lost but searching, for a father, for direction, for justice, for peace. To tell his story in connection with brothers of the past is to autobiographicalize our current generation. Johnson and Shakur are one in the same for many reasons, but the one we can put our hands on is that the community conditions and social forces of both men's times coincide with one another. Social systems create people so Shakur and Johnson are similar because their worlds coincide a certain crossroads and inevitably depart in others. RL's world had black-on-black crime of which he was a victim, but the 1930's black community probably could never imagine the slaughter house of black-on-black murder that now exists.

For us twenty somethin' black brothers and sisters, Pac's shinning path stands as a crucible, a crossroads that we now stand at in our travels into our own futures. We stand mid-road now looking east, looking west, wondering the direction of the wind and the paths of similar spirits. Here in California we have come as far West as we can possibly go. Some of us are headed South, back through Austin toward Atlanta in reverse of our comings in the earlier part of this century. Some say we seem to be in retreat. To others our remigration is simply an inevitable move back home. We have been crossing rivers and roads here for a while, so where are we going? In this maze of directions, Tupac appears and taunts us, beckons us, pleads with us, "All eyez on me."

It is unfortunate that Tupac Amaru Shakur's death now serves as an hour glass through which we see our personal and public pasts. Sifting through the sands of his life and death may reveal the meaning of our time and travels here in the Americas. In his music, Tupac continuously alluded to his death and his only fear: reincarnation. But the question is not will he be back for he will not. The question is *will we be back*, at this same crossroads where the son of the-sum total of our struggles dies by the hand of another of our sons. The question is what will we glean from this and will the wheat of our gathering yield enough to get us over Jordan this time?

"All eyes on me," he said. Tupac's last will and testament: "Look at me, watch this." His fourth album in retrospect seems like instructions, a warning of things to come, of lessons to be learned if we would but "look his way". The event he wanted us to watch was not his death in Las Vegas, it was and is his life, his time(s), his travels. We look to our past and his presence as fuel to the fire of progress. But until we learn these lessons of history, we will always be the crossroads traveler, reincarnated selves with similar shoes; people at the fork in the road, bipolarized by other's beliefs, looking East, looking West, moving South, fleeing North, with our backs to the wind, head over our shoulders, trying to find the river Jordan with a map of directions written in a foreign language, visions of former selves on our trail, and hell hounds at our heels.

The Benediction
Ain't no way overnight to turn your life around
And this ain't the conversation of someone
who never falls back down
But no matter how long you've been on trail
With the days and weeks of self-denial

And no matter how many times you've tried to make it
If you're looking for a loser who found strength and success
Remember the spirit of Brother Malcolm X
And know that you can leave all your mistakes behind
The day you really make up you mind
Really make up your mind
Really make up your mind

Stand up and say
Don't give up
It's time to stop your falling
You've been down long enough
Can't you hear the spirits calling
Yeah, its the spirits
can't you hear it?
calling your name
calling your name
Yeah its the spirits
can't you hear it ?
Spirits

--Gil Scot Heron, "Spirits" from the album *Spirits*

Author's Note:

Orisha-- A general term for a diety in the Yoruba Ifa Divinition belief system. Each orisha has a specific set of characteristics and responsibilities (i.e. ogun is an orisha associated with battle)

Elegba-- An orisha who is considered to be an intermediary between the earthly realm and the spiritual realm. Often mentioned as the diety of the crossroads because of his positioning between the two worlds. Elegba is usually physically-depicted with a double mouth signifying the importance of his communicative role and his double-talking trickster personality.

THE END

by dream hampton

Having attended dozens of funerals for young Black men in the past ten years, most of us must admit a certain numbness to violent death. It should shock us. Leave us outraged. Motivate us. Instead it leaves us exhausted. Spent. Empty. And while, like a lot of women across the county, I was reduced to heaving sobs for the loss of Tupac Amaru Shakur, what's settled in its place is the calm that comes when one has completed an incredibly suspenseful novel. A sigh of relief is breathed. Finally, the drama-- the roller coaster ride-- is over. A chapter closed, the myth that was Tupac can rest in our collective consciousness, to be resurrected when we want to tell our children of the phenomenal and turbulent Black boys.

Pac was that rare creature--a born star. His mother must have known this when she would read headlines condemning her and her pregnant self as she lingered inside a jail cell, accused of conspiracy. And she was conspiring. The Creator and her body would produce a storm. And he would whip us around, change course indiscriminately, target large objects and like all forces of wind dissipate into the heavens. She named him Tupac, after a beheaded freedom warrior, that the original Tupac would enter the Spirit world headless seems particularly significant to our Tupac, who in his last days seemed to have buried his higher self altogether). His name also meant snake and any fan, journalist, friend or family member quickly learned that Tupac was slippery and capable of spitting poisonous venom. It frustrated us. So many of us wanted him to commit to something, anything-- to give his magnificent existence real meaning.

Because we are a generation who has made and lost millions in the billion dollar crack industry, because we are a generation that has buried our boyfriends and girlfriends-- bodies riddled with bullets, because we are a generation who calls the devil by his first name, a generation who created a chaotic musical revolution to serve as the soundtrack for the end of a violent inhumane millennium, the elected few that represent us, in the most synonymous sense, must necessarily embody the contradiction, frustration, passion and fire that is us. That was Tupac's destiny, and he fulfilled it. And in doing so his death has to signify the end of some very useless shit. On one level that means retiring the inane battle between the coasts--which generally bores fans to tears anyway. With it we should hang up our obsession with all things Italian, be it families, clothes or designer houses. We should burn all copies of DePalma's *Scarface* and leave the pile of melted plastic on his doorstep (not so much because he gave our pathos character but because he managed to illicit the most obscure accent ever from one the most brilliant actors ever). We need only to canvas our own rich history to find uncompromising heroes and sheroes. Several that come to mind belong to recent history and they happen to be Shakurs-- the brave, slain Zayd, Mutulu and Assata-- all freedom fighters with their honor and courage in tact, more real than any movie. Most importantly we must work across generations to develop an agenda and then we must live that plan to the fullest. If we are not willing to accept the challenge we must pass the mike--backwards or forwards--but we must move on.

Death is final. And life is for the living. A chapter closed we must do what Pac never did-- choose one or the other.

REFLECTIONS ON THE LIFE AND DEATH OF 2PAC: "KEEP ON LIVIN'"

by Derrick I.M. Gilbert (aka D-Knowledge)

In an attempt to understand the meaning of Tupac
Shakur's life/death, I conducted twenty-six interviews
with a cross-section of African-Americans during the
immediate weeks following Tupac's death. This essay
highlights and synthesizes many of the sentiments
expressed by these twenty-six individuals. My interview
data suggests that Tupac was a complex individual
who intrigued even those who loathed what he
represented. Too, these "reflections" suggest that
Tupac symbolized the contradictions and
shortcomings of rap/hip hop, as well as its
creative, positive and "revolutionary" potential.

I.

After learning of Tupac Shakur's death, my impulse/response was to find out what other people were thinking/feeling about this tragic event. Then, the sociologist in me came out, and I decided to informally interview a small group of individuals to determine how they interpreted Tupac's life/death. Initially, I planned on interviewing no more than ten individuals; however, after reviewing my field notes, and after transcribing audio tapes, I (quietly) realized I had interviewed twenty-six individuals-- the number of years Tupac would have lived if he had made it to his next birthday. Interviewees consisted of: four junior high students, four high school students, a fourth grader, a high school teacher, three college/university students, a graduate student, a fifty-five year old janitor, two university professors, a film director, an actor, three rap artists, a juvenile probation officer, a secretary, a seventy-three year old retired bus driver, and my Mother. All of the interviewees were Black/African-American (choose your nomenclature), yet they represented a broad cross-section of ideas, beliefs and epistemologies. There was no formal structure to these interviews; essentially, I free-styled-- letting the interviews flow. Although my study draws on a small sample, and although my interview schedule was not methodically rigid, I believe my findings are relevant, salient and even generalizable.

Not surprisingly, the comments I received were as diverse as the people I interviewed-- and as complex as Tupac himself. There is no need to quantify how many people spoke positively, negatively or indifferently about Tupac and/or what he represented. Moreover, given space restrictions, I am unable to elaborate on all of the themes presented, and I am unable to include quotes from all twenty-six interviewees. Thus, the interview data used in this essay represents only a small portion of what I collected.

II.

If there was a general theme that connected the twenty-six interviewees, it was a theme of intrigue. Whether Tupac was liked, disliked or viewed indifferently, my interviews reveal that almost everybody was intrigued and compelled by this rap icon. Even those who were most critical of Tupac, and even those who loathed everything he represented, still found something "fascinating" about him. A Women's Studies/African-American Studies professor told me that:

> I'm not going to say that I'm glad he's dead--
> that would be sick and mean-spirited. But
> I do think that [Tupac] pumped a lot of venom
> into our communities. Now, I understand the
> forces that created a Tupac, but I still hold him
> accountable for perpetuating violence and sexism
> in our communities. And, you know, it's a shame
> because he had so much charisma...and he had
> such a powerful presence that he could have
> actually helped turn things around.

This professor's statement characterized the view of many of the "non-hip hoppers" I interviewed. That is, the "over thirty" interviewees were intrigued by how much the youth were intrigued by Tupac. Thus, a thirty-two year old actor would say:

> Tupac didn't necessarily strike a chord with me.
> I mean I liked some of his work like "Dear Momma."
> But he didn't really mean anything to me. You
> see, I'm an adult and I already made it over the
> barriers of being a young Black male. So I wasn't
> concerned with Tupac. But I was fascinated at

> how he struck a chord with our generation,
> with our future. Tupac spoke to their realities,
> not mine. And so I often listened to his lyrics
> in order to feel the pulse of the moment.

For those over thirty, then, Tupac was a symbolic representation of a (hip hop) culture that they knew little about--a culture that they were generationally removed from. Moreover, they were fascinated with how Tupac "lived on the edge" and in how he constantly "danced with death." Again, they did not necessarily understand Tupac or "connect" with him, but Tupac did tickle their curiosity.   Perhaps this had to do with people's peculiar fascination with death. After all, many of the top-rated television shows in this country revolve around themes of death or virtual death (e.g. *Homicide, ER, X-Files, Millennium*, ad infinitum). But Tupac was not a television show-- he was real life (or, as it would play out, he was real death).   Tupac was our nephew, our younger cousin, our student, our younger brother, or even our son. That is, Tupac was an ubiquitous reality in our communities and in our lives--even for those of us who did not care to admit it.

III.

The younger interviewees, however, did not need sophisticated sociological or psychological explanations to explain why they were intrigued with Tupac. Most of the younger interviewees echoed what a thirteen-year old junior high school girl told me:

> I just liked Tupac. I don't know why-- I just
> liked him. And when he died, I felt like a
> friend of mine died. He just did that to me.

Of course, some might suggest that the media and promotions/marketing directors influenced "how much" today's youth "liked" Tupac--and there is certainly much truth in this assertion. However, Tupac effected and affected our youth in a visceral way that cannot be exclusively explained by the media. Which is to say, Tupac (himself) played a significant role in the equation, because his was an organic (not media-contrived) image that fully connected him with a bewildered and jaded generation.

Indeed, a seventeen-year old high school senior highlighted that:

> The muthafucka was me. He lived what I live.
> Even when he got paid, he still had to worry
> about the bullshit-- you know what I'm sayin'.
> He wasn't no fake nigga talkin' about he was
> from the 'hood-- that nigga lived what I live...
> that nigga got shot livin' what I live. So, hell yeah,
> Tupac meant a lot to me.

Not only was Tupac perceived as being real, he was also viewed as knowing how to overcome pain. In other words, despite everything Tupac had gone through, he could still smile/he could still dance/he could still get paid/he could still get high/he could still live. Thus, another high school student told me that:

> Shit is hard out here, you know. I'm trying to
> go to school, but I got all kind'a shit to deal
> with at home and out here on these streets.
> And Tupac dealt with the shit too, you know
> what I'm saying? But Tupac didn't just talk about
> thuggin', he also rapped about havin' fun--
> you know, havin' a good time and shit. Sometimes
> you just gotta say fuck it, and that's what Pac did.

IV.

During the course of my interviews, I noticed that Minister Louis Farrakhan was frequently mentioned. Actually, several interviewees directly implied that Tupac shared a similar symbolic space with Farrakhan. When I first heard this parallel, I thought it was somewhat awkward. After all, Farrakhan, I reasoned, is a distinctly political figure who is ostensibly dedicated to a "moral, economic, and spiritual" cleansing of Black America-- while Tupac was more about "fame and gettin' paid." I then realized that the parallel had little to do with the content of these men's lives, and all to do with their public representations. Thus, whereas many people do not "agree with" or "like" Minister Farrakhan, most Black folks either respect him or-- at least-- acknowledge his captivating charisma. Of course, I am not implying that Tupac was a hip hop counterpart to Farrakhan-- that would be a silly analogy. Instead, I am simply suggesting that, not unlike Farrakhan, Tupac had a presence and a charisma that attracted the attention of even those who disliked him. For example, a thirty-six year old secretary and single mother said:

> Tupac scared me! He represented everything I don't want my 8 year old son to grow up and be. But, in a strange way, I do hope my son has the same courage as Tupac. Not the stupid gang kinda courage, but the courage to stand up for what he believes. It's the same way I feel about Louis Farrakhan. You know I get very upset with many of the things Farrakhan rants about, particularly since my mother is white...but I also respect that he says exactly what's on his mind. And, although I don't want my son believing those kinda things, I do want him to have the boldness to say what he does believe in.

Further, a twenty-three year old Oakland rapper said:

> [Tupac] kept his shit real. I mean, he might have been one of the boldest Black men around. That nigga told it like it is. Now Ice Cube and a lot of them other niggas are bold too, but none of them is bold like Tupac. Most rappers, and most niggas, are soft like Jesse Jackson and shit. But, Tupac was hard like the Minister [Farrakhan].

Tupac, then, was viewed as a defiant voice (and symbol) in a country that is still viewed as hostile and unjust to Blacks-- and particularly Black men. Like Farrakhan, Tupac was a heroic symbol of resistance and rebelliousness. For today's Black hip hop youth, Tupac became their Nat Turner/their Sojourner Truth/their Marcus Garvey/their Malcolm X/their Angela Davis/their icon of rage, resistance, and struggle. Of course Tupac did not articulate the same "political themes" as the aforementioned, nor did he seem to be working for the upliftment of Black people; however, he did represent the quintessential rebellious spirit through which today's Black youth can vicariously live-- simply by watching his videos, listening to his CDs, or by conjuring his image in their minds.

Although there are a lot of rappers who are respected and adorned by today's youth (e.g. Ice Cube, Treach, LL Cool J, The Fugees), none have intrigued them quite like Tupac. A parallel from another historical moment, and from another social/cultural milieu, might be Evil Knevil. After all, in the seventies there were a lot of daredevils, but there was only one Evil Knevil. Similarly, although there have been a lot of magicians/escape artists, there has been only one Harry Houdini. Tupac was that one bold, intrepid, assertive, charismatic, crazy muthafucka in the rap game. Tupac was the one who lived his life on the edge/who had played games with rats in dilapidated projects/who saw his "dear momma" go from Black Panther to Black Crack Head/whose flesh had been penetrated and scarred with a plethora of bullets/who had painfully contorted his body on concrete-hard prison beds/and who had prophesied his own death. Oh yeah, Tupac was the one.

V.

The question now becomes, what's going to happen to Tupac posthumously. And, perhaps, more importantly, how is Tupac's death going to impact the rap world and-- by implication-- hip hop culture? Well, in a relatively short time span, rap has already undergone tremendous changes. Of course, Black folks have always been rappin', but most of us agree that it became a "commercialized" genre with the release of Sugar Hill Gang's "Rapper's Delight" in 1979. Since then, rap has rolled through our communities (and the world) collecting all sorts of debris. Thus, for example, today the lyrics of Sugar Hill Gang, Grandmaster Flash, and even Run DMC seem rather simplistic compared with the intricate word play that is apparent in such rappers as Nas and the Fugees. However, where the craft has developed, and where the styles have rapidly expanded, the content has perhaps digressed. There are, of course, several exceptions to this, and perhaps KRS-One and Chuck D epitomize the positive/creative possibilities in this genre, but both of these rappers are in their thirties and no longer have the same appeal as a Snoop Doggy Dog or a Biggie Smalls-- or the rap flavor of the month.

Not to be lost in the discussion of the change, we must also acknowledge the market forces which have significantly altered the parameters of rap. After all, despite attacks from Bob Dole, Newt Gingrich and other political (Republican and Democratic) elites, rap is now a multi-million dollar business that has been co-opted by the deceptive/manipulative power-brokers in the recording industry. Thus, rap is a new species in an ever-evolving (or devolving) society. But somehow we must "de-commercialize" rap, and bring it back to the communities from which it was born. This genre is too powerful and too important to be corrupted by the business. When I was coming up in the mid to late eighties, Public Enemy and Boogie Down Productions helped foster my cultural/intellectual awakening. Unfortunately, today's rap does little by way of educating and uplifting our youth; in fact, it often perpetuates such destructive concepts as misogyny, xenophobia and--perhaps most frighteningly--nihilism. Here, I borrow my understanding of nihilism from Cornel West, who describes it as:

> ...The lived experience of coping with a life of
> horrifying meaninglessness, hopelessness, and
> (most important) lovelessness. The frightening
> result is a numbing detachment from others
> and a self-destructive disposition toward the world.
> Life without meaning, hope, and love breeds
> a cold-hearted, mean-spirited outlook that
> destroys both the individual and others.

However, I am optimistic that rap can become an ingenious weapon that eradicates the nihilism in our communities. But we need to have faith in rap, and we need to respect and nurture those who are involved in it. I agree, then, with playwright/poet/novelist Ntozake Shange, who says that:

> Actually, I felt-- and still feel --that I have the
> same connection to rage as [the rappers]. I also
> feel that the rappers are very passionate, and
> that revolutions are ultimately built on passion.

Again, I emphasize that we must nurture, cultivate and help channel this passion. If we lose faith in these talented/creative individuals, and if we attack them more than we love them (ala C. Delores Tucker), we will witness more degeneracy/more vulgarity/more violence/and more nonsense. But if we do support and encourage the passion, if we do caress the revolutionary potential and spirit in rap, we might very well observe the rappers liberating us.

As for the effect/affect of Tupac's life/death? Well, I think Abiodun Oyewole, an original member of The Last Poets, articulates my sentiment best:

> With the Tupac thing...I think some kids are going to say: "well, if you play in the traffic, you're going to get hit." That's how many of us will view it—it's just a nonchalant view of life. And Tupac will be glorified by some kids—somewhat like Jimmy Dean is with white boys. You know, Jimmy Dean was a rebel without a cause—and Tupac was a rebel without a cause. Tupac didn't really represent a cause, other than the public madness between the two industries: the left coast and the beast coast, as far as I'm concerned... There's nothing really that serious that we should be fighting over, because none of it is ours in the first place. In fact, the game is not even ours to determine. So it's sad now, but I think that hip-hop is in a strategic place, because it has the ears of a lot of our young people today. hip-hop can still make the strongest impact among the youth, and I think it can be a very strong instrument to change a lot of the negative attitudes and the negative activities that have been taking place under the heading of hip-hop. I think that hip-hop can actually transform itself into something much greater and much more productive than what it is. But right now it's in the confusement park more than it is in the amusement park. It's kind of sad in many ways.

VI.

By way of conclusion, I must say that, when I heard that Tupac had been shot (this final time), I optimistically hoped that this incident would be the wake up call he really needed. Although I conceded that he had been given several previous wake-up calls, I really wanted this shooting to be the cold water in his face, waking him up from a twenty-five year nightmare. Even when I learned that

Tupac had lost a lung, I said to myself: "NOW this brotha can take his craft/his life to the next level." After all, my logic followed, "if Tupac really changed, millions of Black youth would be inspired to do the same." Unfortunately, Tupac did not live (although several of my partners tell me he is still alive...alas, a Black Elvis); sadly, he did not live long enough to grow/change/influence others to do the same. But I constantly think Tupac Shakur could have been that one-- that one resourceful rebel with a cause/that one courageous cultural warrior in the struggle for equality/that one truth-giver in a world full of lies and liars/and that one "down brotha" in a community overwhelmed with bourgeois, pompous and aloof "leaders." Tupac could have been the one...multiplied by many.

VII.
Finally, I recall my last conversation with Tupac, in which he told me to "keep on doing your poetry, man--we really need it." In retrospect, I wish I had told him: "Keep on living, man--we really need you." Of course, my statement would not have changed the course of history or the course of Tupac's fate; however, it would have been important for me to have told this extraordinarily talented, charismatic, potential-laced brotha: "Tupac, keep on livin', man, 'cause your life means more to me than your death."

Notes:

i   Cornel West, *Race Matters* (Boston: Beacon Press, 1993), pp. 14-15.

ii   Taken from an interview I conducted with Ntozake Shange, which will be published in *Catch The Fire: A Cross-Generational Anthology of Contemporary African-American Poetry* (New York: Riverhead/Putnam, 1997).

iii   The full interview with Abiodun Oyewole (of The Last Poets) will also appear in *Catch The Fire*. See previous citation.

iv   I last spoke with Tupac Shakur a week before The Las Vegas shooting. The conversation occurred at the *Comedy Store* in Hollywood, California.

2
verses from the underground

HARDCORE

by wadud

This is for all those supposed hardcore hip-hoppers
hoppin' round on one leg in the wrong direction
bein' spoon fed the notion
that Blk on Blk crime is somehow sexy
that if you look like you can kill somebody
u ain't got to be able to do it
but if u look like you can kill somebody
then you all that

imitation base sounds destroy
blk boy creativity
turn them into pistol whippas'
of family members and
there is no deeper meaning.
imaginary talent recycles young folk
over and over
with a hip-hope life span of
2.34 records
booooooom bip

but him was real bop
on the cover of rap weekly
baldheaded with a snarl of spit
hanging from his lower lip
financially secure
synthetically angry
his job was to keep blk boys pointed
toward prison.
so him dressed like convict
or at least him was told to dress like convict
cause that's what sold records
incarcerated clothing
droopy jeans
oversize backwardness
with draws showin' IQ sizes

and learned symbols of power
strapped to the front of his pelvis
they said:

> you be sexy if ya' hardcore
> if you could stroke a girl while
> drinkin' a 40 and
> bus' a cap in her temple
> while stabn' yo' brother
> in a video dream.
> *put a gat in yo' mouf fool.*

so he called himself sexy man
bigdaddy allpenis
da' mac machine
moneymaker g-love u too much
bitchnigga afrikan.

him wore a medallion with
misspelled words
a cold-blooded x curl commercial
for young people to follow
and white folk to exploit
he had a chain saw in the projects
like a blk gimmic with no trees to cut
the negro rapper boy wanted the world
to believe him out of his mind
so he get respect from other people
who beeeeezzzzzzz stupid
but u see
the SOURCE of hip-hop flows from
the pockets of white folks
tellin' us what they'll spend their money on
and what they won't:

> ok lil' blk boys
> we'll pay for images
> of anger and lack of self-control,

so when we split
some of your baldheaded skulls
we'll be able to justify it.
now stand over there wit' this
beer bottle and blunt in yo' hand
and say "cheese"
so america's most wanted poster
can match your album cover.

u see
when u own the circus
when u come up out the pocket
and pay for the circus
the clowns have to dress the way u
want them to dress
or they can't perform.

no other group of people
would allow their children's images
to be portrayed as
something so insignificant.
death row is da' label dat' pays me...
watch the trick

u can dance now

UNTITLED

by Toni Asante Lightfoot

Sick smiles dance
at the death of a thug
who lived confusion
spoke out both sides of
his consciousness

Street life's high tide rolled
swept 5 bullets into his body
left him one testicle
to teach how fragile
manhood can be
lessons unlearned
come back on the final exam
4 lead questions
stole his breath
his soul eaten by
the gods of the street
this time he could keep the
gold
tattoos
record contract

He prophesied on MTV
to keep it real
he needed to get deeper
into the gansta shit
chose to cliff dive
into the abyss of show
and fell six feet

Memorial services
held in packed houses
of God
brothers and sisters
waited in line

as ministers
joined in the chorus
the rhetoric
in the end
nobody
could bring him back
nobody really wanted to

Self-exploited
Tupac has become
the anti-martyr

INNER CIRCLE

by Jenoyne Adams

When you wear your rag on your mind
drenched in mama's blood and examples from
half-ripe penises with blue-black balls
bangin' and slangin' and stuffing eight barrel
shotguns up the anuses of little black gods
watching them explode into thin white lines
for Uncle Sam to smoke
leaving their dicks and faces
hanging on his walls like milk carton trophies

when God is a wounded G.I. Joe action-figure
stylin' purple cowboy boots
flinging an umbilical cord lasso
to strangulate his posse

when your woman becomes a bestial black-bitch
a receptacle for the world's cum

when black is the uncensored enemy
and you've been enlisted
to annihilate your self—

you're fighting the wrong fucking war.

WHERE WILL OGUN LIVE?
(FOR THE TURMOIL OF 2PAC)

by AK. Toney

Where will Ogun live in a world full of niggas?
on the sixth step of maroon colored stairs
on the corner wit' an iron pipe pincher in right hand
and an eye-full of gangrene plumbing rage in the other left
where the first flame lights the color of spring
traps the soul into darkness
for show of glow from ever-essence
alone in the forest

i sit and put in work on corners
asking Elegba
what Ave.-blvd.-St. should i take?
i put the pistol close to my tree
and hope the hole i shoot through
is the sap of my honey
ashe.
ashe! is the *itations* of thik smoke
like rolled tindu leaves equivalent to cigars
orisa like monkeys on my back
as nigga runs in Ghede guerrilla camouflaged warfare dance
i should cut a tattoo in my heart
when cold blood runs warm
like life no longer exists
i jump into stab wounds permanently carved
jiggy-chek chants
pop scars in the spirit
i animate love unconditional
'cuz of lack of prayer
of lack of power
...of lack of prayer
but where can a babatunde lay his legs and rest his head?

Where will Ogun live in a world full of niggas?
in the House of Sampoerna 234
from Indonesia where the cloves r so sweet
that u withstand heat of the spark...
in Salem lot where tobacco is grown and weaved into fonta leaves
like a noose wrapped around smoked necks...
in a Newport misty hole...
still live with pleasure!
on a Camel's hump too heavy for the ride
'cuz i think too much...
in doja bush where smell of green is too potent to be lit...
(and if Marlboro was a blak man saddled on a dog with a
double-edged ax, who would Shango be?)
in volcano where i worked with Shango's father
and i smythed my machete and swords and knife
while he produce seed of lightening...
i am hunting for u corner.
i am hunting in Kool breezes of menthol and solid spontaneous
combustion from Garcia y Vega since 1882 before the freedom of
slaves and beget that
ashe.
ashe!
ashe! i burn with the anger to kill the Master
i question to spare the slave
i will stand on one-time justice from bullet burns bleeding
around gun-powdered uniforms.
but where will i live?
what good am i to the civilized world?
where will i live?

WHO WILL BE THE LAST POET?

by Jessica Care Moore

This piece was originally written for Umar Bin Hassan of The Last Poets and now I give it to the memory of Tupac Shakur and poets across the globe. Remember our purpose is to live.

Who will be the last poet?
Paying dues to prove we know it all
I'm saying toward the East salaat/praying
We're gaining inner peace treaties
Smiling with silver spoons on boxes of wheaties
Eating bowls of sacrificed lambs
Cooking our craft like Sam
I was born by the river
When pure water deteriorate your liver
Giver of ghetto voice
Machete Mouth grenade
Everyone sips your spit adding flavor
To their piss-colored lemonade
Crazy ace of spade
Speaking in twisted scattered Scorpio speak
Outsiders search for leaks
Hate to see you at your peak
Fake winks blown away with swift brushes of ink
Compete for props
Blow up the spot
Freedom fighter
Revolution inspired
Liars wisdom on wasted energy
Trying to see me
Boomeranging unfounded breaths of negativity
What you hate about me
You hate more about yourself
Wealth cannot buy self-love
Bloody gloves
Fit finger pointers
Anointers of analytical arguments

Flared
They were the first to tell us
Niggas are scared
E Equals M-C squared
So why do your lyrics lack
Well-rounded energy?
Root of spoken trees blown away
As we smoke weed
Drinking herbal tea
Defining me
With plastic score cards
Compromising without realizing
This used to be a movement
Political platform
Means writing poetic porn
Getting some revolutionary ass
On the college dorm floor
Deep in the heart of Harlem
Spirits and sporadic microphone sex
Test the status quo
How many poets gotta go?
Who will make it out
Before we choke on clout
Greed and sweaty palm
Pimps and prostitutes
Make the best poets
Hustlers and hijackers
Convicted felons
Thieves stealing watermelon seeds
From kids at picnics deserve
Pulitzer prizes
Literary recognition
For being literally what they claim to be
Cutting down cherry trees
Unafraid don't flee
Poets sitting on santa's knee
Wishing for a war we could win
With a ball-point pen

Ink blots block out the true meaning of life
Poets packing guns and bladed knife
Kill the voice
Chock-holding heroes
You get a zero
For owning mental locks without roots
Tongues that shoot blanks
Yanked from the ranks
UN honorable diss-charge
Without purple heart
You the man today
Gonna blow up this cafe anyway
M-80 toting lady
Drowning your selfishness
Beneath the Euphrates
I'd rather trade these young hands
Gripping glass
Black girl juice dripping down your throat
So you can taste what you could've had
Sad Spiritual schizo
What a poet know?
How low can we really go?
When the ego self destructs
Like plastic legos
Who'll build evil empires
Poet for hire
You're fired
For not continuing the legacy
One of the first quenching
Hoodlum thirst
Holding educator and politicians
At pen point
As we steal truth
Tracking our arms with addictive scars
Cause our people have been fiending for centuries
Your voice always so clear to me
Please stop all this madness
Please stop all this madness

For our poetic fathers
All seven
It's the 11th Hour
Poetic showers don't always wash off mud
Shoved between crippled African toes
There goes
One more, two or three
Nothing worse than a slave free
Killing his own family
Forcing tubes down throat
Can't forget what you wrote
Don't you ever float...float on!
Till the break of dawn
Poets are being born
As we speak about the art form
Pregnant with metaphors, music, moonlight
And microphones

You are our open door
After a long walk home
Your stones skip rocks and wave to wannabees
Trees bow their knees
Wooden broomsticks wither and cry
Cause they lost the chance
To sweep you off your feet
Repeat!
Who will be the last poet?
Show it off
Your sexy big red "S"
Poetically undressed your lyrics are skinny
Carved like thanksgiving turkey
Your breasts are juicy
But the milk is stolen
Swinging swollen fists
Miss every time
My words are wind
Blowing past you
Can't kill original rhyme creators

You brought rhythm and revolution
Extinct like eagle
Soaring into the souls of black folk
Live what you wrote
Write while you're still alive
How many will die?
For the last chance
Complacent with southern comfort
With no proof or poetic license
Rolling dice and shooting craps
Against concrete curbs
That elevate us above the earth
Still remaining grounded
There are shoes to fill
On the long walk home
So we adjust our tongues
Tie our young laces
Races end up at the starting line
Time is not finished
So throw your hands in the air
Above your heads
For old times sake
Take your manhood and lie it face down
On the cold cement
Check it in Black poet
You are well read books
Hard undercovers
Language lovers
Turning truthful page
Raging rivers rescue real revolutionaries
Cause even water gets thirsty
Returning to the well
Throwing pennies into black holes
Wishing words were worthy of our expression
We have leaned since the first day you decided
To show it
Not everyone will make it out alive
Who will be the last poet?

A Poem for Cowards

by Derrick "Goldie" Williams

Everyday I see coward ass niggas
Posing as authentic gangbangers
Talkin' 'bout they got stripes
Their acclamation to fame is shooting a black man
But are any of these so called gangbangers
Willing to use their guns in the revolution?
Are any of these so called gangbangers
Willing to empty the clips of their 9 double m's
For the liberation of black people?
Cause to me
You ain't a true gangbanger unless
You gangin' up
and bangin' up
on the real gangsters
Operating incognito as representatives of a democratic society
Imitation gangbangers *set tripping*
on other imitation gangbangers
Not realizing that the real set trip is on those
who have set you up for failure
Booby-trapped your quest for success
and tripped you to fall
Deep into a black hole of self-destruction
Nigga, will you *set trip* for millions of Afrikan ancestors
who died in the Atlantic slave trade?
Will you and your posse, get into your Chevy
And *ride down* on American hypocrisy?
Are you willing to *represent* Black Power
So brother Malcolm's death will not be in vain?
Nigga would you bogard for control of your own destiny?
Are you going to organize your homeboys
Into a clique of freedom fighting assassins
All across this continent?
'Cause if not,
Get the fuck out of my face.

TUPAC SHAKUR

by Brooke Oden

We all thought we knew him
and we did
very well.
Not by personal acquaintance,
of course.
But from the News
Top 20 Countdown,
his albums.

His boastful tone
made friends and foes
If you were male,
you either
quoted him
or envied him.
If you were female,
you were either
offended
or wanted to sex him.

Whatever the impact
he'd made on you,
there was an even greater one
as soon as you heard *it.*
Word-of-mouth
is swifter than airways.

Unbelievable.
It really was.
It is.
His first survival
had made him
immortal
so he thought
so we thought.

Dead at 25
Dead?
The King of lyrics,
loot,
and ladies,
Never.

But it's true.
And here lies
the proof
that he wasn't a 'studio gangsta'
and what a price for such proof.
Thug *LIFE*?

LAMENT FOR BROTHERS

by Glenis Redmond Scherer

too soon
too soon
death comes around
too soon
like winter's night
snuffing out
the brightness
of spring shining
in your eyes.

The dull ache
of mourning
attaches to us
like tree limbs
that won't shake
words that will not
be written
music never
played
heavy air
carried
held
in tight fisted
scowls.

We
know
black men leave
this world
too soon

We are
empty wells
filled with grief
with the memory
the music
of you.

TOUGH LOVE

by Kwame Alexander

I remember
Charleston...

we hopped clubs
cruised ghetto heavens
smilin' and discussin'
rights and plights
of menchild
in broken promised
lands and
later
she approached
for an autograph
but instead
joined u in the stall
for a 10 minute
lesson on oral sex with a
condom
while the homies
guarded
yr throne
and laughed
when u
came
out

or was it
NY...

where yr name
evoked unfocused power
in the souls of
powerless youth
who saw
yr achievements

as indication
that dreams
cd come true
even if
u refused to
wake up and
then u died
a cruel and foreshadowed death
leaving us
receipts
and lyrics
contradictions
and questions
that can never be answered

In the coming days
yr role as gangsta/prophet
will be played
over and over
by countless understudies
staging action
seeking identity
stealing vision
and *we*
who understand why?
you were a "thug-4-life"
will
measure
examine
and score
our direction of your lessons
mapping your complete existence
with a critical compass
pointing somewhere
between
tough
and love

3
gathering witnesses

WHO KILLED TUPAC SHAKUR?

by Charlie R. Braxton

In the absence of an absolute truth about the murder of Tupac Shakur, many people attempt to fill the void by proposing countless theories as to who may have killed him and why. Theories range from the plausible to the straight up imbecilic, but very few, if any, examine the critical socio-political issues that ultimately lead to the conditions surrounding Shakur's death. As a result, the root cause of Tupac's and countless other young people's deaths go largely ignored.

In order to fully understand Tupac's penchant for the thug life, it's important that we understand some things about his life prior to his landing a recording deal.

Tupac Shakur was born on June 16, 1971, to Afeni Shakur, a former member of the Black Panther Party who was jailed for her alleged part in a plot to bomb several public places in New York.

While pregnant with Tupac, Afeni spent several months in a women's correctional facility. She was released a few months before Shakur was born. During the early part of his life, Shakur was shuttled from place to place, sometimes staying in homeless shelters. During this time frame, Afeni was relentlessly harassed by the police and FBI so much so that Tupac would later tell a reporter that he saw his mother get interrogated so often that he thought her first name was "Black Bitch." Later on, Tupac had his own run-ins with the law.

In early 1986, Afeni was introduced to crack-cocaine by Leggs, the man Tupac adopted as his father. Tupac was enrolled in a local Harlem theater class where he excelled in dramatics. Later, the family moved to Baltimore where he entered Baltimore School for The Arts studying drama and ballet. In June, he and his family moved to Marin City, CA where he was introduced to the "Thug Life" of petty crimes and drug dealing.

America Eats It's Young

According to statistics, Black men are six times as likely to be murdered as white men. Murder is the fourth leading cause of death for Black men between the ages of 20 and 29. Homicide is the major cause of death among Black males between the ages of 15 to 24. 84% of all violent crimes committed against Blacks are committed by Black offenders. Black men make up a disturbing and disproportionate number of our nation's prison population. And the numbers go on, as does the criticism of the gangsta rap genre that

Shakur has been publicly associated with.

Most notable of the critics are C. Delores Tucker, Melba Moore, and the Black conservative columnist Armstrong Williams whose "I-told-you-so" tone now permeates the media.

"His death was tragic," writes Williams in his syndicated column published just after Tupac's death. "But it does not change the fact that Shakur surrounded himself with violence and lived the life of a thug. [He] was victim of the street violence perpetuated in his gangsta rap."

But the real question of who is ultimately responsible for the real life violence that takes place in our streets each and every day, robbing our communities of their happiness...their sanity...their lives, Williams and the rest of the rap critics ignore.

We need to ask ourselves who is more responsible for the deplorable systematic criminalization of our communities. Is it Tupac and his gangsta rapping cronies who sell millions of records laced with gritty tales of drugs, murder and mayhem, or is it other more sinister forces that preach family values in public and practice the exact opposite in private. And lastly, could some good old-fashioned family values alone, save the Tupac Shakurs of America.

The late Dr. Amos Wilson, noted African American psychologist and author of the book *Black-on-Black Violence* offered some interesting views on these questions when I interviewed him two years ago.

"You see you've got a lot of people who want to lay all of this [Black-on-Black violence] on family values and the absence of some kind of old time religion and things of this nature. And while that's a part of the mix, you cannot just blame this all on the loss of family values. People don't eat values you know. You have to actually work, you have to feed your family. There are concrete material things that people have to have. And so the mere training of people in family values is not going to solve this problem. As a matter of fact, when you transform people's material position in the world, you transform their values. So a part of the transformation of the values that we complain about is a result of the transformation of the concrete living conditions of black people."

Black-on-Black violence that is gripping our community, the same violence that killed Tupac, Mr. C of the RLB Posse, Scott La Rock (remember him?) and countless other Black men, women and children, is directly tied to the rampant white supremacy and poverty that has held a death grip on the so-called Black underclass in this country. It is also strongly tied to the influx of drugs, particularly crack-cocaine, shipped into Central Los Angeles by what the San Jose Mercury News reporter Gary Webb alleges were CIA-backed operatives, who were involved in the distribution of the poisonous product through the entire West Coast and many parts of the Midwest and the deep-South via the L.A. street gangs known as the Bloods and Crips.

Many criminologists and community activists around the country agree that with the advent of the crack trade, violent crime increased significantly in Black & Latino communities around the country as the two gangs began to fight bloody wars over drug turf.

It is no secret that poverty, drugs and rampant violent crime go hand-in-hand. Where one goes the others are sure to follow. Any kid living in the ghetto can tell your that.

And while rap critics such as Tucker and Williams may argue that Tupac was a millionaire when he died, they conveniently overlook the fact that Tupac and Death Row President/CEO Suge Knight (a man who makes no bones about his alleged affiliation with the Bloods street gang) were from impoverished backgrounds, as are many of Shakur's fans . It is as the age old adage says, "You can take a brother out of the ghetto, but you can't always take the ghetto out of the brother..." at least not in the small amount of time that Tupac had to adjust to going from pure poverty to superstar millionaire.

While this writer will be among the first to admit that Tupac made some bad choices in life and that the hip-hop nation needs to be more responsible for the images that are projected before our children and the world, I'm certainly not the one who will simply dismiss Tupac nor any other Black or poor person of color's death as just another case of you-live-by-the-sword-you-die-by-the-sword murder. It's much more complicated than that.

The world that Tupac once lived in and rapped about so passionately in many of his songs is the same world that claimed his life, but bear in mind it was a world that he neither created nor controlled. Tupac is not the father of the white supremacy that is the root cause of the vehement self-hatred in the hearts of millions of Black, Brown, and Native American ghetto dwellers in this country. He didn't create monopoly capitalism which is largely responsible for the debilitating poverty in our community. Nor did he ship tons of cocaine and guns into a social tinder-box known as the Ghetto, be it South Central or anywhere else. To blame Tupac and the gangsta rap genre for his murder and the violence that takes place in the society at large, and not condemn the socio-political forces that continue to drown our communities in the blood red sea of drugs, guns, poverty and despair, is a classic case of blaming the victim. That will, in the end, get us nowhere.

Tupac Amaru Shakur, the self-proclaimed "thug-for-life" is dead. His name now joins a growing list of young black males and females whose lives have been needlessly cut short by violence that is an essential part of American culture.

In that sense, his death, as was his short but promising life, becomes a bitter reminder that for poor Black and Latino youth life within the confines of these American shores "ain't nothing nice." It never has been and, if we don't wake up and create a serious movement for positive social change, it never will be.

A Two-Pack of Tupac

by Marsha Mitchell-Bray

My homegirl in Vegas called immediately after news reports broke in on her regular programming to announce that 'Two-Pack' Shakur has just died--" calling him "Two-pack" as though he were dual rolls of tissue paper wrapped in some kind of plastic shroud.

As his death began to hit L.A. news stations, I was still incredulous. In my mind, I had confused the man who had been spun on the wheels of steel since the beginning of my college days—with the Teflon don of comic book fame. You know, the man of steel, big "S" stretched across his chest, able to leap tall buildings in a single bound, bullets ricocheting off him.

It was easy to see why the two morphed into one, after all Shakur had survived being shot five times by sewer rats trying to get at his jewels and countless scrapes with the law. But as reality began to creep into my consciousness and I acknowledged his death, my extremities went numb. I went into a catatonic state.

Standing on the periphery of the LA hip-hop scene, I'd seen Tupac all over town—at clubs, at the listening parties of various artists and even on Venice Beach. As a writer for *Rap Pages* Magazine, using the pen name the "Empress of hip-hop," I had even dissed him in my column for his ill behavior towards sistas. And though I belonged to the industry, I still wasn't prepared for my up-close and personal meeting with the man himself.

It happened on a Friday night at "Juice," a club then housed in Carlos and Charlie's Restaurant in Los Angeles. As I hung out with other *Rap Pages'* staffers, we witnessed the last act of a drama which ended with Tupac being taken into custody by the police. Apparently, Tupac had punched an overzealous female fan in the nose because she was hounding him for an autograph. What was so strange about the episode was that after it happened, Tupac stood outside calmly smoking a spliff as though nothing had happened. I mean home boy out-calmed Hannibal Lector after having a human liver with fava beans for lunch. Tupac showed absolutely no remorse or emotion. When five-o showed up, he got in the car without saying a word as the girl he punched watched.

A month later, I was asked by my editor to do an interview with the rap icon. I had serious reservations about this interview for obvious reasons. But still, I was very excited about the prospect of an interview with Tupac Shakur. So what kind of sista did that make me? Talking out the side of my neck, I had often spouted rhetoric about weak negros who put their hands on sistas as a means of feeling powerful. Meeting with my crew of sista/girls, I talked about how African American women had to make men respect us by steppin' off if we weren't treated right. And in conversations with strong, positive sisters, I bantered about the need to love ourselves. Yet, despite my black feminist posture, I was getting my hair done and donning my best hottie gear for a question and answer period with a misogynistic, card carrying member of the "He-Man Women Haters Club". And yeah, I'll admit it. I wanted him to find me attractive. I wanted him to sit and smile at me as I asked questions. In short, I wanted him to jock me.

Still, I wondered if I could keep my disgust under raps over the incident I had partially witnessed. I wondered if I could remain objective. I wondered if upset by my questions, would he punch me in the nose too?

I knew no matter how I felt about Tupac and his antics, his music spoke volumes to his fans, of which I was one. If it offended some, it did so in the same way the sight of a lady of the night catching a beat down from her pimp would. If it inspired you to think, it did so in the same way that Malcolm could electrify a mind. If it inspired you to take a stand, it did so in the same way Dr. King made the nation get up and take a stand. If it educated you, it did so in the same way Huey's Panther School in Oakland gave knowledge to the black, disenfranchised masses. Thus, I decided to put my neck rolling in check and pressed onward.

As I approached the plush conference room of Death Row Records, Tupac's mother, Afeni Shakur, stepped to me—a protective mother-panther ready to pounce. "Who's the Empress," she asked in a take no prisoners manner. I hemmed and hawed and said, "due to confidentiality clauses I cannot release the identity of the Empress."

I knew full well if I told her I was the Empress she'd never let me conduct the interview. She hit me with a "momma know you lying" look and let me into the room. And there he sat, in all his b-boy splendor. Hat to the back, diamond earring sparkling. He stood up and introduced himself. I took his hand, told him my name without looking directly in his eyes and sat down.

Getting my tape recorder out, I finally made direct eye contact. To my surprise, the Tupac I expected was totally different from the brother who sat across from me. He was absolutely beautiful. And I'm not talking about the fact that the man was fine.

He was beautiful inside and out. He wore a beautiful expression; not the one customarily seen on album covers, in magazines and videos. But an expression that was welcoming and sincere. His smile lit up the room. His intellect beamed with brilliance and his love for his moms shone apparent from underneath a boyish grin which gave his face character.

I was taken aback. How could this be the brother who had played the role of "Bishop," a little too convincingly in Ernest Dickerson's film *Juice*? How could this be the brother who physically assaulted women without regret? How could this be the man whose lyrics, on many occasions, had offended my femininity?

In the course of our hour-long interview, we talked about everything from video games to D.C. politics. He was candid. He was truthful. He was open, wide open. There was no knuckle up-and guard-your-grill tension. There was only Tupac.

I found the answers to all my questions. And I, ironically, discovered that the media had not been all that wrong in the pronunciation of Mr. Shakur's first name. He was a "two-pack," if you will, because he existed in dual roles in the drama he called his life. And the act of maintaining this duality was as delicate as tissue paper.

The first role was that of street warrior turned thug which he portrayed and paraded in front of video and movie cameras, on records and around the rap industry's top impresarios. Biggie Smalls figured out Tupac was playing the part of "Bishop" off-screen after witnessing him jump out the back of a limo at a music awards show and yelling out "Westside gangsta."

And why shouldn't that have been his premiere role? He said he was the hybrid cross of "a black panther and a street hustler." And it was that role which guarded, no, protected his secondary role of intellectual, philosopher, social activist and formally-trained dramatist.

In the aftermath of his death, the media and old heads that make up the generations of our parents and grandparents have forgotten to remember that Tupac was very intelligent. He was educated at the Baltimore School for The Performing Arts. He was a philosopher able to pen songs like "Keep Your Head Up." He was a social activist who flexed his ability to deliver social commentary on songs like "Brenda's Got A Baby." And he was a formally trained dramatist, able to switch modes from the psycho-killer he portrayed in *Juice* to the vulnerable lover opposite Janet Jackson in *Poetic Justice*.

Unfortunately, and for the most part, young black men in our community do not value the intelligence, philosophical insight, social activism or formal training of which Shakur had an abundance. So he hid that side of himself, freeing it occasionally in the songs that touched our collective ethos. To put it more plainly, in a time where to like school is to be considered soft and where perceived social leaders are not to be trusted, the life affirming role that burned so brightly within Tupac was destined to always be at odds with the self-destructive gangsta role that youth glorify.

Slowly, thug life won the tug-o-war with the Black Panther inside of Shakur. Starting in 1992 with the assault of the autograph seeker and continuing in 1993 with the alleged shoot-out with Atlanta police officers; the 1994 arrest in Hollywood for weapons charges; the 1994 15-day county jail stay after attacking film director Allen Hughes on a music video set; the conviction in October 1994 of misdemeanor assault and battery charges in Michigan; the November 1994 incident in which he was robbed of $40,000 in jewels and shot five times; the February 1995 sentencing to four and a half years in prison for sexual assault and ending with his murder in Las Vegas, thug life claimed a generation's gangsta prophet— leaving the rest of us to mourn the Panther.

As I came out of my catatonic state, I asked myself who had really died? What part of Tupac was murdered? Was it the talented young producer/writer/entertainer who had beat the odds and made it to the summit of success? Or was it the gangsta with the "bitches and hoes" mentality? And if so, how could I, as a woman, cry for him?

As I mulled these questions around in my soul more than in my mind, I suddenly realized it wasn't the gangsta, who hit and sexually assaulted women, that I was mourning. Therefore, I had no reason to feel guilty about my grief.

In that moment, I understood that I cried for Tupac because I am the mother of a young black male and I know the pain his mother feels over losing her only son to violence. I cried because another young, black male voice had been stilled. I pined because our ranks had once again been violently depleted.

Checking the clock, I found that my revelries had lasted two hours. My husband had picked up our son, Malik, from the sitter's and was roughhousing with him on the living room floor. As I looked at my child, I wondered if he too would succumb to the magnetic pull thug life seems to have on young black men—despite the upbringing my husband and I will give him.

Malik will go to Marcus Garvey Elementary School—a black-owned, founded and managed school. He will attend a private high school and then go off to the college of his choice. And just as Afeni Shakur taught her son, I will teach Malik why it is necessary to be socially active and stand up for the causes in which he believes.

Like Afeni Shakur, I will hone my son's creative, artistic and philosophical talents. Like Afeni Shakur, I will teach him to be the social chameleon I believe every African American becomes when they venture out of their neighborhoods in order to attend college or punch the clock on their nine-to-five. And like Afeni Shakur, I will wonder if I have given my son enough skills to survive the duality of his existence.

PART-TIME THUGGIN':
REDEFINING A GENERATION BY DISCARDING THE THUG SWAGGER

by Frank Williams

> *"I wonder if heaven got a ghetto for thug niggas,*
> *a street life and a spot for drug dealers"*
> *—from Tupac Shakur's* "If I Die 2Nite"

Once, when I was still determined to give props to the pool hall hustlers that raised me on crack-crazed corners in east Oakland in the 1980s, I decided to call my first volume of poetry *Notes From Behind the 8-ball, Poetic Verses from an Intellectual Thug.*

It seemed, at the time, the only appropriate way to truly capture the dualities is that nourished me from wide-eyed toddler to manchild B-boy. But after a lengthy self-evaluation and seeing so many dead "thugs" on the news and in my own hood, I saw the fallacy in thinking I should hold on to the false notion that I could simultaneously act as a warrior for black babies and still be a part-time thug. The light clicked on in my head one day: as much as thugging was in my bloodstream, shrugging it aside was too.

That is the greatest lesson I take from the tragic shooting death of my brother, Gemini soulmate and fallen comrade, Tupac Amaru Shakur. I must for the duration of my life, follow my gut in defining the real nigga outline of my soul. Life is too short to let others do it for me.

Perhaps that is the saddest part about Tupac's death-- he refused to follow his instinct, which he said repeatedly told him to let "Thug Life" go. I wish he would have shaken it off, so Tupac the actor, poet and budding black nationalist could have taken over.

I can't *playa-hate* him though. I've done it a million times myself. Tried to live up to other folks expectations and definitions of how I should be and act.

Tupac was one of the clearest snapshots I have ever seen of my own wayward generation. At times, the black twentysomething crowd can be fearless like him, other times utterly inane and self-destructive.

My first knowledge of Tupac was from his early days when he rapped with another MC named Ray Luv in the Bay Area. But it was in college that I really discovered him. Though I went to college and Tupac to the streets, we still shared a common frame of mind: always be down with the thugging, but pray and work towards peace.

We both had grown up in intense and often violent crack-addicted homes. We both fled to our creative passion-- words-- to escape ghetto drama. It was as if Tupac had tapped into me, like the still-opened veins that dope fiends were always searching for.

His first album, *2Pacalypse Now*, still ranks as a classic hip-hop ghetto ululation in my head. The beats were whack, but his talent shined through with his uncanny ability to capture the realness of the hood's hope and desperation. This was when his lyrics were about something more than death, sipping Cristal champagne and toking weed.

He sported African beads, rhymed about unconditional homeboy love and pointed fingers at my own teenage nemesis-- The Oakland Police Department. There is a distinct anger Tupac and I likely developed during our teenage years in the Bay Area, where even when you tried to be conscious and down for a peaceful struggle, the police seemed to have it out for a young nigga. It probably stems from the long-standing history of bad relations between black people and police in the Bay Area, especially in the overlooked blue collar city by the Bay.

The Black Panthers had many famous run-ins with the infamous Oakland Police Department, which my uncles always told me was just the latest chapter in a divided racial saga in our city. I imagined Tupac being inspired by the same environment, it providing ink for his pen, inspiration for his alcohol induced rap flows.

Every time I heard *2Pacalypse Now*, which touched on themes of black male insecurity and even teenage pregnancy, it reminded me of my own internal battle to stay on the so called righteous path. I always told my boys that I was just a few steps from a jail record like Tupac. With all the scuffles and excessive drinking, I was just a few minutes from letting the built-up anger from my own childhood explode. But the eventual difference between Tupac and I was not only the fame, but that I simply refused to let the anger take over. I now know there are other channels for my fury. The fire inside had to be contained and used at the right time and aimed at the real enemies.

I've finally realized that "keeping it real" is being true to black progress and not embracing thug behavior. Shooting at other brothers and calling women bitches is not an accurate portrayal of the person I am or want to be.

Why are some brothers afraid to stand up and say thugging is wrong in any form? Why can't we expand and then redefine what a real nigga should be? Why do black folks alienate themselves from ways or things they think are supposedly un-black?

Since I have jammed on many late nights to the amped up sound of the rock group Nirvana and know the lyrics of some Duran Duran songs, does that make me less of a real nigga? Am I less down with black upliftment if I think "Thug Life" is backwards? Even Tupac quite frequently mentioned his love for the writing of Shakespeare and appreciation of other styles of music.

Maybe Tupac couldn't heed his own call for self-liberation. Near the beginning of the song "If I Die 2Nite" an announcer says: "A coward dies a thousand deaths, a soldier dies but once." When I die I want motherfuckers to say P-frank represented what we really need-- a black nationalist that loved having fun and getting busy, but respected himself and his people.

Living like a soldier for black people means making sure you are in a position to help the cause. Atlanta rap group G.O.O.D.I.E. Mob was right when they said: "See to me, a G' is a person who understands the plan/ can't do nothing in the hands of the man." Tupac couldn't do nothing for us when he was locked up for nine months in an upstate New York jail cell. There should be no cool points given to cats who are on lockdown. Obviously brothers and sisters who are victims of police frame-ups are different, but any person who truly believes that jail is inevitable is wrong. Any nigga bragging on jail, like a few of my own homeboys, is wrong, and like thousands of brothers in jail, only hurt their families. Dead men, especially dead thugs, do little for us except provide memories of when they were here on Earth. As my homegirl said days after Tupac's death: "Everybody knows that thugs either end up in jail or dead."

To say I did not shed tears for Tupac would be a lie. In fact, I cry often when I realize how many of us are being wasted everyday all over the country. For weeks after Tupac died, I played the song "So Many Tears" until the CD was scratched and I had to go out and buy a new one. It only proved that after four years of writing stories about slain gang members (mainly black and Latino males) I too wanted to drown my sorrows in green sacks of cannabis or use bottles of Seagram's Gin to numb the pain.

It's easy to try to define ourselves in the Big Willie dreams of Lexus cars and Armani clothes. All those videos showing brothers with guns tucked in their jackets and sisters dancing around in tight vinyl pants make us think that in order to be "the man" you have to be perpetrate like a studio gangster, that you have to be down with some lightweight thugging to be real. That shit ain't true. Like Nelson George says, "a studio gangster can't out rhyme a bullet."

A true soldier knows separating himself from the traffic of negativity is more difficult, yet more valuable to his race and himself, than shouting "Fuck The World."

I now have a distaste for thugs. It's not like I've become a young conservative or I'm saying some curse words are out of place, or insisting that hardcore rap is futile. I'm just tired of thugs fucking up my groove at parties just when I was about to get the number.

I am not there yet. As my mid-20's finds me in constant change, more sooner than later, the thug in me will be gone forever. I wish it could happen for every nigga I know, but unfortunately there is still too often a willingness for brothers to think that identifying with the criminal, the thug, is what we are supposed to do.

Perhaps it sounds juvenile or stupid, but I wonder if Tupac went to heaven or hell. Growing up, my elders were always putting the bug in my ear. "Boy you going to hell if you keep getting into trouble," my grandmother would say.

And if there is a heaven, then we should set ourselves up for a proper landing by our actions here on Earth. That means being true to yourself no matter what the crowd says. I'm not the best of role models, spending many nights bent off alcohol, searching for car keys and talking shit. But there was a point when I realized that all the posing and trying to live up to the definition the media has carved out for us (as out of control, angry black men) is pointless.

Turn off that television and radio, African boy. You ain't no thug and I ain't one either. And if I'm not mistaken, real bad boys move in silence.

We can identify with the thug's pain, but we don't have to be the hard rock to be seen as a real man. 'Pac, with all this outlawesque behavior-pushing brothers in crowds and spitting in the eye of the cameras (OK I secretly dug that shit)-- couldn't let "Thug Life" go.

That "Don't Give A Fuck" attitude most thugs have is what paralyzed Tupac. And his need to live the life of the "Black Scarface" is what ultimately killed him. I hope that is not the legacy of his valuable life; of this generation of young black men.

We need a few more full-time black men and a lot less part-time thugs. For the brothers who are still here, there's plenty of time to escape the trap of internalizing anything close to a thug mentality. Free your mind from all the drama and peep the bigger picture. If you don't you'll be wondering, like Tupac did, if God has a space reserved for you.

Rest In Peace Tupac Amaru Shakur. We praise your passion. But "Thug Life" deserved to die.

Waiting For The Future: The Death of Tupac

by Tony Medina

> When my heart can beat
> no more
> I hope I die for a principle
> or a belief that I have
> lived for
> I will die before my time
> because I already
> feel the shadow's depth
> So much I wanted to
> accomplish before I
> reached my death
> I have come to grips with
> the possibility and wiped
> the last tear from my eyes
> I loved all who were positive
> in the event of my demise
>
> *—Tupac Shakur*

This is not a eulogy. Nor should it be mistaken for one. The day Tupac Shakur died from gunshot wounds sustained in a gauntlet-like drive-by shooting, he did not become a martyr for a generation with its much exploited and maligned creativity and culture. Instead, like O.J. Simpson and Mike Tyson, he became not just another American made high tech statistic, but a metaphor, as well. When, sadly enough, Shakur was pronounced dead on September 13, 1996 (ironically the 25th anniversary of the Attica massacre-- see note), he became a metaphor for the frustrated, confused, divided determination of a generation of angry youth whose revolutionary potential had been torn away from them with their umbilical cords at birth.

In this whirlwind year, which eventually claimed his life, Shakur was served with a 120 day sentence for violating his bail (at the time of his death he remained free pending an appeal); he completed two films: *Gridlock* and *Gang Related*, two albums: *the don killuminati: The 7 Day Theory* (under the pseudonym Makavelli) and *One Nation* (which is an attempt at squashing the East Cost/West Coast rift).

What we see here in this final combative and turbulent year, is not only the artist as a young man working feverishly to pump out new work as if-- like Coltrane before him-- he had a premonition of his own impending doom, but some one finally making the move away from the personal and political vacillation that tangled his mind and weighed him down. Shakur, in this instance, had proven himself to his peers and his fans by "keepin' it real." He proved to the record industry that he could sell records and generate income. He proved to the movie industry that he could be a professional actor, meeting his appointments, showing up to work on time and cooperating on the set. And finally, he proved to the powers that be that he was an artist who was able to reach not only black youth, but white youth, as well, with a message (although conflicted and confusing at times) that spoke to their level of apathy and disdain for a system that is indifferent to their plight and suffering.

But the mature Tupac Shakur was never allowed to surface. In an interview (probably his last) with Rob Marriot for *VIBE* magazine, Tupac said:

> *I tried to see if it was, like, a white thing. Everywhere I go with money, they let me in. Everywhere I go with none, they don't let me in. Trust me. That's all it is. It's all about money. When you got money, you got power. I guarantee if people keep supportin' me-- just buyin' my records, just goin' to my concerts-- I'ma keep givin' money. Every time I go platinum I'm puttin' money up for community centers. Every time I go platinum, somebody's gettin' a big check. I feel like an elected official.*

In this interview it is clear where Shakur was headed.

> *You know what I thought when I was in jail, I was like. No politician is gettin' at us. I represent five million fuckin' sales. And no politician is even checkin' for us. But by the next election I promise I'll be sitting across from all the candidates. I promise you! I'ma be so far from where I am now in four years-- God willin' I'm alive-- it's on! I guarantee we will have*

our own political party. It won't just be for
blacks. It's gon' be for Mexicans, for Armenians,
all you lost-tribe mutha fuckas. We need to
have our own political party 'cause we all have
the same mutha fuckin' problems. We built
this nation and we get none of the benefits.

It is no great political revelation, nor does it take any deep philosophical waxing to claim that record companies and media conglomerates make money off of the suffering of poor people and people of color, and that these same forces make money off of promoting the backward and detrimental genre in hip-hop known as "gangsta" rap. (Did they not introduce blaxploitation films and drugs into the community to undermine the Black Power Movement in the late '60s and early '70s?) Like crack and heroin and AIDS (and any other genocidal design) manufactured and distributed for our detriment and demise and their profit, the backward element in hip-hop music will be produced, promoted, and supported by those who control the purse strings. Those backward tap-dancing, soppy jheri-curl wearing coons that act as corporate officials-- sucking rich white ass and gyrating before a video camera-- will, no doubt, continue to exploit "gangsta" rap (like the petty drug running slaves they get to sell crack to kids and skinny people with sad, distorted baby faces). And, as in all art forms, there must be a battle waged, a sort of class struggle between the positive and the negative, between the backward and the progressive. This occurred nearly 10 years ago when Public Enemy burst upon the scene to put the ideas and image of Malcolm X on the hip-hop map and snatch the Apartheid-South African-gold chained mentalities from rappers personas.

What is most telling about Tupac Shakur is that he, more than anyone, embodied DuBois' profile of the dualistic black psyche in white America, and derails it into the 21st Century with the on-going problem of the color line, which continues to justify the system of monopoly capitalism.

> *I am crazy. But you know what? I don't give a fuck!*
> -Tupac Shakur as "Bishop" in *Juice*

Shakur, it seems, believed in his own hype. He was caught up in the fantasy world of Hollywood devil-may-care make believe irreality. Clearly, this is a throw back to the '70s blaxploitation films which satirized black militancy as buffoonery and perpetuated the image of the crazy nigger. This could be seen by his thug life campaign, which, he claimed, was greatly misunderstood. Yet he initiated the confusion. It was his distorted view of what black manhood was that emerged from the persona he created. As an astute black youth interviewed on BET perceptively claims, "He died because he created his image; and his image killed him." And though poignant and haunting these words may be, at second glance they are slightly off key because capitalism is also to blame. It plays an important role in manufacturing and perpetuating images of what black manhood or humanity is. It is capitalism that lures and recruits our youth from the projects and ghettoes and suburbs alike to fit and fill the mold it has created. And our youth, rappers and non-rappers alike, have ingested the capitalist ethos of competition and greed and dog-eat-dog mentality. This fucked up world out-look also has its roots and tentacles in the world of drug dealing/hustling and that of gang membership and involvement because it is these elements that have been socialized to emulate and imitate the capitalist-- the man: he who has the money and the power, he who calls the shots, makes shit happen, kills people even. This is why the Mafioso lifestyle and persona as portrayed on TV, the big screen, the 11 O'clock news and in papers is so popular among rough-neck, wanna-be-gangster, hip-hop types. These images of man-hood and womanhood have been so distorted throughout the post-'60s, post-Nixon/Reagan/Bush years that they have created the East Coast/West Coast rift, that has instigated the gang land violence that exists among the Bloods and the Crips.

For anyone who consciously fights against this beast we call America, con-stantly feeding its belly with our young-- especially those of us who are of Shakur's generation-- it was frustrating to know that a son of the movement could come out strong against capitalism and politicians and police; in defense of young black men and praise black women in general and his own troubled mother in particular-- while at the same time rap about bitches and hos, espouse thuggishness and gangsterism, perpetuating these ideas and images in song, in film and in his own real life drama lived out on the 6 O'clock news along with the other statistics they parade around for white America's titillation and trepidation. And even though Tupac Shakur made you sick at times by the dumb moves he made or the stupid shit he sang or said, like our version of a Farrakahn, you knew deep down that he'd one day make that permanent leap forward to clarity and maturity.

Tupac Shakur's death leaves a stale after taste for generations who remember Freddie Prinz's suicide, Marvin Gaye's murder, Jimi Hendrix's overdose and many other artists and cultural icons who died too soon. 'Who killed Tupac?' will find its place in American popular culture along with: Where's Jimmy Hoffa?

Is O.J. guilty? Who shot J.R.?

In the final analysis, I believe that Tupac Shakur's death is an extension of the long arm of COINTELPRO that literally told his mother's generation of militants in the '60s and '70s that not only will we get you, but we will get your children and your children's children. This can be seen by the state of our youth today: the uneducated, the drop outs, the unemployed, the imprisoned, the coerced (who are lured into a life of dealing drugs such as crack cocaine and receive stiffer sentences than white yuppies selling or taking cocaine), the forgotten, and the constantly criminalized. This can also be seen if we consider the fact that rap (a grass roots art form, revolutionary from its inception) makes its entrance onto the world stage on the heels of disco music and the blaxploitation era which undermined and replaced the Black Arts Movement and the Black Power Movement. And, interestingly enough, it was born at the same time as AIDS; rap and AIDS are the same age. Ten years later as rap begins to become more popular and profitable, broadening into the hip-hop culture and so-called nation, crack is infiltrated into communities of color by the CIA (recruiting and employing drug dealers and gang members and using the profits to bank roll the counter-revolutionary Contras in Central America), gang land violence is on the rise, and AIDS continues to kill like a fire out of control. At the same time, political rap (the original hardcore rap) emerges on the hip-hop scene, hangs tough for a while, and is quickly stomped back down by big business and small-minded criminals.

Out of all of this, and out of the troubled life of a post-DuBoisian black-psychical dualism (the illegitimate son of a hustler and a revolutionary-turned-crack-addicted mother far removed from the political consciousness and discipline which shaped her), Tupac Shakur emerges like a meteorite or a ball of flames full of his own confusion, contradictions, apathy, frustration, and rage. He was a reluctant Icarus, both impatient and waiting for the future to make his final move, only to get his wings caught up in the cross fire of the sun's violent consuming branches and its merciless rays.

Author's Note:
On September 13, 1971, New York Govenor. Nelson Rockefeller ordered the suppression by force of a prison rebellion in Attica Correctional Facility. Prisoners, demanding basic human rights, took guards hostage and barricaded themselves in the prison yard. The National Guard was called; after tear gas was thrown in, they opened fire, killing 43 people, including 11 guards. The prisoners harmed no one.

Black Males and Suicide:
America is Driving Them to Death

by Omar Tyree

> *"Can't stop, won't stop."*
> *"Do or die."*
> *"The beef is on."*
> *"I'm going out strong!"*

...Battle cries of young black suicidal hit squads across America. They think like kamikaze soldiers, fully strapped, steel-eyed and ready to kill or be killed. Sure enough, according to the National Institute of Mental Health, during the last decade, 1980-1990, blacks between the ages of 15-19 and 20-24 had the lowest suicide rates among young American males with numbers of 11.5% and 19% respectively, as compared to 19.3% to 26.8% for young white males, and 13% and 20.6% for all other nationalities. Young African-American males, however, approach suicide in a different way. According to Sonya Donaldson, a licensed clinician at the Psychiatric Institute of Washington, DC, "a lot of the depression is expressed aggressively. And they involve themselves in situations where they don't care if they live or die."

For them, everyday is a mental battle on this red, white and blue land which they feel trapped in because their brown skins reflect the African heritage of a rival red, black and green. So now, many young black men, with their youthful energy, have turned their daily strife into a desperate need to fight and die. Why? Because there continues to be few places for strong black males to showcase any recognizable skills in white America outside of entertainment and athletics. And many are too rightfully proud to accept that daily dosage of demeaning workplace racism that says that they are less than. Therefore, the hard-core streets have become their only sanctuary, their only family and their only interest, even if it includes dying.

Author Sanyika Shakur, in his book *Monster: The Autobiography of an LA Gang Member,* says, "Though never verbally stated, death was looked upon as a sort of reward, a badge of honor, especially if one died in some heroic capacity for the hood. The supreme sacrifice was to take a bullet for a homie." He adds, "life meant very little to me. I felt that my purpose was to bang. My mind-set was narrowed by the conditions and circumstances prevailing around me... Where I lived, stepping on someone's shoe was a capital offense punishable by death."

There are more than one hundred area "crews" in the District of Columbia. The homicide rate continues to escalate past record numbers. Needing more answers, I called DC's 24-Hour Crisis Line, part of the Emergency Psychiatric Response Division, to discuss the problems of those young black males who call in for help.

"A lot of them are suffering from peer pressure, pressure in school and disunity in the homes," Tony, an anonymous mental health advisor, said. "Sometimes it's like pulling teeth to get them to talk. But when they do, they usually have a lot to say. They just need somebody to listen... Then again," Tony added, "A lot of them don't call."

Since my arrival in Washington, DC in the fall of 1989, the nation's capitol has battled to remain the "Murder Capitol" of America. So I guess there still is a whole lot of listening to be done-- and fast! But once you start "banging" it becomes hard as an addiction to quit from fear of "punking out."

Backing down from a confrontation can make one, in male philosophy, seem like a girl. Now the last thing a stressed-out and angry young black male wants to hear is his peers referring to him as "a bitch." That is a big difference between male and female peer pressure-- men have been forced to put their lives on the line to protect their manhood, their families and their societies. Truth is, many new generation black males view the previous generations as cowards. And it keeps getting rougher and rougher as we approach the twenty-first century.

"My mom used to tell me, If you can't find something to live for, you best find something to die for," said the very political and controversial, Tupac (RIP). He tried to hold fast to his family's Black panther roots and the militant creed of dying for revolution against "the system of the man." Tupac said in a Premiere magazine article, "The fact is, unless I want to turn into an uncle Tom, I will be a statistic. There's no way around it. Unless I want to turn my back on what's going on in America, I will either be in jail or dead or be so fuckin' stressed out from not going to jail or dying or on crack that I just might pop a vessel. All the deaths are not going to be from the police killing you," he continued, "it could just be the stress you go through from being black in America."

However, this "us against the man" creed does not exempt one from killing any and everyone else who may step wrong. But as Malcolm, Huey Newton, Nat Turner, George Jackson, Eldridge Cleaver and may others have already proven, there can be a very fine line between criminal minded suicide and die-hard nationalism. In fact, black verses white tension remains the specific problem that creates black on black violence. Blacks have learned to displace their anger on a much less intimidating foe, themselves.

One thing that does seem to lessen the despair that drives young African-American men to suicidal extremes is that of full artistic expression and compensation via entrepreneurship, music, movie-making, acting, writing and developing new black cultural bases. It takes courage and confidence to stand up to peer presure and express oneself as a black man in white America. In many cases, though, it's those unexpressive, quiet types who are most effected by environmental stimuli. They become the hardest to reach because they realize that in this land, black male expression often equals death, especially for those who are uncompromising. It's "do or die" in everything that young black men think about. They "can't stop, won't stop" until they become the survivors that they're going to be-- or die.

When I was in high school, my friends figured I was suicidal because I expressed stress differently. I was one of those overachievers that always took situations to the extreme. I often felt that I was supposed to win, that I was supposed to be successful, and that I was supposed to fulfill whatever I wanted to accomplish in life. So I took failure hard, and I still do. But I've learned to turn failure into stepping stones. And I still feel that I will win. I don't have any "beef" and I'm not going out on any suicide missions. We have work to do, a culture to build, dreams to fulfill and children to raise. As a Black man in America, I will show my son, Ameer, that a brother does not have to follow suicidal tendencies. He needs a daddy; a black man who knows what time it is; a black man who plans to see him grow old; a black man willing to help him survive the American system every step of the way; a black man who is not suicidal.

Embracing Our Confusion:
Lessons About Black Womanhood

by Jiton Sharmayne Davidson

> *Thinking all of her life that her suffering was for*
> *a higher purpose; that she was to grow and*
> *become some pivotal piece to some great*
> *puzzle made it like the last dying when she*
> *found out that she was just for feeding...*
> *Nourishment for layers of the world that*
> *needed her richness. Like the soil that thought*
> *it was the seed. Generations of trees, dark,*
> *smooth, bending against the white blizzard.*
> *Growing heavy with strange fruit. Growing*
> *strong and knotty because of her.*
>   *from SISTER, MAMMA, GIRLFRIEND*

Breast to mouth, and soul and soul. Black woman has always been for feeding. Before the passage, before stretched drums warned of invasion-- annihilation, before the passion fruit in the garden and blame, Black woman was for feeding. How much of herself did Afeni give to her son & to the nation & to the struggle & to the street-- Black Power. How much of themselves have sisters given to Tupac and Black boys with money and fucked-up messages about her stuff-- her thang--the way she shakes it-- the way she educates-- the way she mothers & nurses & loves. Black womanhood has provided a feast to the hungry soul looking for someone to blame for his life-- his death. Tupac fed. Tupac fed off of the hope for an authentic voice fostered in victims. He fed off of victims who in turn fed off of his poison-- a self-destruct cycle. Tupac, like many young Black men, was a victim-- of collective stupidity. This stupidity makes a messiah out of a lost little boy shouting "...put yo' mouf on the pistol;" makes a sister hate herself, her brother/man; makes a boy want lots'a bitches to prove his manhood; makes a sister go down on a gangsta' on a dance floor. Tupac was a little Black boy in a big scary world that paid him to sell his people self-destructive prophecy-- feeding off of the dignity of his sister, mamma, girlfriend.

We say it's just music, 'I ain't trin' to be no role-model.' We say it's just music-- words that help us let go of the shit that is killin' our spirit, but in a very specific way *it* is the shit killin' our spirit-- the unified African-American spirit.

Self-destruction. History is a muthafucker whose unused lessons will get you again and again until you learn them-- or go boom. History can tell us why Tupac punched a sister just for asking for an autograph and why he married a long-time girlfriend in jail; it can tell us why some women are so worthy of disrespect in the eyes of Tupac and many brothers like him, and why he worshipped his mother-- all Black mothers. History can tell us why Tupac's confusion about Black women marked an evolutionary step in the right direction. History is a mutha' fucker, but if we remember we can save ourselves from choking on the bile of regurgitated lessons never learned.

History's Lessons About Black Womanhood

This is not a rap lyric but it is on the real.

When the first Africans were brought to America in 1619, a security device was implanted so deeply within the universe of their collective consciousness that they would carry on the work for destruction of the Black race even after their slavers went into hiding. Let's say a group of oppressors conquering a new land wanted to assure that their subjects were controllable, mutable and accepting of their treatment, under very economical terms. Let's say these oppressors planted this virus whose objective is to aid in the destruction of this used and discarded community of people by attacking the core-- Black male/female relations.

making sense?

Let's say they start by destroying positive and desirable images of the woman, the one who gives birth to the future. Let's say they call her breeder, winch, mammy, ugly and every time you turn on the TV about 300 years later, you are infected with the oppressor's ideals of her worth. And then your Black queen mutates into a brother emasculating, sell out to the race, white dick wanting, bank/lexus motivated, crack/welfare ho.

...and some where around the end 'you wonder why they call (her) bitch.'

It used to come from the slavers, now it comes from us. We all fight it-- try to love ourselves. Brothers fight it. They look at their sisters, mammas, girl-friends and say "of course we are not calling all Black women bitch and ho." Inner conflict is good. It means we are evolving. The lyrics of our tragic brother Tupac emphasize the internal conflict that many young Black men carry about Black womanhood. They are our dear mammas, our hos.

thank God for pussy, huh?

In our eagerness to be victims no longer, we sometimes forget that our history still affects us in very real ways. If we can keep these things in mind... If we can say Brenda is a ho because... If we can say there is a wedge between us because... If we can find the origin of the sickness, we can cut off the supply of poison and heal ourselves. We can disarm this self-destruct sequence if we pay attention to the evolutionary track and effect of dissin' Black womanhood.

...your heart...

In the early days of African-American history, Black woman was the key to the unraveling of the Black spirit. She was separated from her man, her children were the commodities that gave her worth, her stuff was free and sweet like paradise fruit. Black men soon saw her as the weak link and the oppressors' collaborator. Practically imprisoned in the big house and forbidden to give her love to the man she chose, Black woman was further alienated from her brother. She was even a betrayer to her children-- birthing them into a life of brutal servitude while at the same time giving her love to the white children she mammied for. Once released from slavery, Black people had already suffered a debilitating infection. Newly free and consummate rejects, the Black male and Black female came together, trying to build a home on the impotent seed of sharecropping and the bitter leavings of a people who hated them.

is it coming back to you?

Following the failure of southern living for the African-American, they migrated to the cities where Black woman was welcomed into the Big house (a place her man was not welcomed) as the maid. Offered welfare and public assistance if she once again separated herself from her man, she was seen as money hungry and capable of doing anything from selling her children, to selling herself to make bank. Literature and later TV reflected her evolution only from the point of view of those in power, white men. While Black writers (in this man's world-- mostly men), when they addressed Black womanhood, tried to love her, they could not get beyond the hurt of this perceived betrayal. His woman not only cleaned up for the white man, loved his children and gave up her man when she needed assistance; she had the nerve to be the paragon of ugly with her nappy hair, large features and dark skin. The sixties brought a more vocal, militant sister to the front:

....afeni...angela...elane...erika...kathleen

And also a low-keyed internal struggle with-in the Black Power movement for, you guessed it, power. She was the emasculating bitch-- the woman saying, sure you can be the man but don't expect me to trade myself off from one oppressor to another. Today some sisters fight back at the wrong enemy by endorsing the one-sided ideas that some Black male bashers sell to us via white owned-publishing houses.

...breathe out...

The animosity that was implanted centuries ago (and now threatens to grow into a huge, god-old, Georgia, hangin' tree) comes out in our sanctioned decimation and parodied portrayals of Black womanhood. But our natural inclination to love each other causes a very pronounced duality in brothers' ideals of Black womanhood. The confusion that Tupac's lyrics reflect, in a loud and strong voice, is a good sign. It means the brothers that he represented see their sisters, mammas and girlfriends in the faces that have been painted as the enemy.

...dear mamma can you save me?

Our Confusion

Who can say Tupac was not conflicted? He promised us all that he would try to follow a more spiritual path once he got out of Clinton Correctional. For a while he loved all of us until "money" in a big car say--

this who you is

--until history said--

look what that bitch did to you

If we can acknowledge that historical animosity is the root of many of the problems between us-- that historical animosity, planted centuries ago can cause painful confusion for a young brother like Tupac trying to love; for a sister trying to love herself-- then in order for us to stop hating ourselves and blaming ourselves, we should examine the current effects. We all accept that the land of a lost people that Tupac rapped about is a reality. With what we now know it will never be enough again to simply say that that's just the way things are. If we apply what we have learned... If we try to understand the circumstances that force some sisters to play out negative roles today (gangsta rap did not invent these images), we may acknowledge that we are a unit-- Black man, Black woman-- and we need to embrace, protect and love each other instead of following our self-destruct programming.

What makes a sister that ho that is the subject of many rap lyrics?

It's surprising and a little disheartening to be a sister who has worked hard all your life to feed your children and get them started on a better life, and to realize that your chances of falling in love with a good brother who loves and respects you, wants to rub your back and watch your back for a change-- are thirteen to one. Thirteen Black women to every one Black man. The most twelve of those women can hope for is occasional love, the most they can

expect is children. Brothers love the vast pool from which they can sample--
even the "good" brothers. They should. They have earned the right as
survivors and the other most important key to the survival of the
Black race.

> How many brothas
> fell victim to the streets?
> Rest in peace my niggaz,
> there's a heaven for a G
> Be a lie if I told you
> that I never thought of death.
> My niggaz,
> we the last ones left.
> But life goes on...
> -- Tupac Shakur, "Life Goes On"

Life can not go on without our men. It's beautiful that we always find a way
to survive. However, some young sisters, crazy from the reality of the staggering
competition, will do anything they have to in order to not end up like their mothers,
lonely and dry from lack of essential love. The best freak is the chosen one.

> Every other city we go, every other video,
> no matter where I go I see the same ho.
> -- Tupac Shakur, "All About u"

But seldom is she the one chosen to marry when it's time to pocreate. These
insecure sisters are the women represented in Tupac's song "Wonder Why
They Call U _ _ _ _ _" (All Eyez On Me).   He addresses her:

> lookin' for a rich man--
> you dug a ditch,
> got your legs up tryin' to get rich.
> I love you like a sister
> but you got to switch.
> And that's why
> they call you bitch.

There is no denying that Tupac was conscious of the different types of sisters and he tried to make that clear. In a world where you are money and every body wants a piece of you-- this kind of sister becomes connected with destruction. Indeed, her sexual behavior can kill you.

right, e-z?

Tupac, in his song, told her about herself-- with love. He even acknowledges that for some sisters, this behavior can be a way out.

...roll to school-- years later you can show them fools...

Yet, even after all of this-- after he praised the mamma ("...dear Mama, you are appreciated") and offered painful, but loving advice to the ho-- he refers to the woman who was sodomized in his hotel room as a woman scorned.

conflicted?

Our Fate

Nobody needs to be told what the African-American faces in the future if we continue to follow the self-destruct programming that eats away at our core by eating away at the core of our male/female relationships. Internally, brothers like Tupac are dealing with the dualities of a society that tells them that they should talk about the "hos" and the "pussy" that gets thrown in their faces daily, while the spirits tell them that Black womanhood is sacred. It's very hard not to go with the flow and do what you've always done.

When the stakes were not so...

When brothers loved themselves as well as their women and children;

When brothers were not giving it up on the street-- their lives, I mean;

When brothers were not housed in prisons-- many times because survival forced them into criminal activity, we could afford to be stern in our loving criticizing of each other-- "this is the way you are and it's hurting us." But now, in many respects our stern criticism of each other grows into huge fists that beat all the love out of our union.

The kingly Black man is leaving us at such a frightening rate that good sisters are turning to other women for that spiritual and physical love that is so essential, good sisters are turning to white men, good sisters have to battle the damage done to the minds of the few brothers left by insisting (quite harshly sometimes, as in Terry McMillan's case) that we are not all ho's and should not be treated as such. It's important to keep it real if we really want to grow...

...but where is the love?

Where is the internal conflict about Black womanhood in Gangsta' Rap?

These artists should be conflicted like Tupac. At least there would be some love. In this case it is wonderful to be confused and even okay to rap about it.

...then get over it and move on.

Our babies-- little boys and little girls-- are not immune to the damage that has been done to the image of Black women. They themselves will have to work through this. If they are only hearing the self destructive arguments, however, their actions will follow as they grow up.

Even white men are fearful of the power that hip-hop contains. Instead of turning this weapon upon ourselves, we can use it to unite. I praise Tupac for his confusion-- a fight for your life from birth makes enemies out of most. All of our brothers are so precious when they bond and fight for survival. But don't bond against me, the one who would give it up for you-- my life, I mean. Don't bond against me-- the one who continues to feed you. If we allow ourselves the luxury of a real and spiritual love... If we pay attention to the past and offer loving criticism while we keep it real... If we embrace our confusion then move beyond it, we will survive as a whole and healthy unit. I praise Tupac for allowing us to feed off of the lessons he left. So what, he didn't get to learn them himself, but maybe his mission was completed anyway.

> *nourishment for layers of the world that needed*
> *your richness...like the soil that thought it was*
> *the seed... generations of trees, dark, smooth*
> *bending against the white blizzard... growing*
> *heavy with strange fruit growing strong because*
> *of you...*

BLACK CULTURE AND 'THE REAL'

by *Michael Eric Dyson*

Near the beginning of Spike Lee's important film based on Richard Price's arresting novel, *Clockers*, a group of young black, street-corner cocaine, dealers, the "clockers," engage in heated debate about hip -hop culture. At stake is who is the "hardest" rapper in "The Game." Public Enemy rapper Chuck D's name crops up, but he and other "positive" rappers are quickly mowed down because they "never shot nobody," they aren't "slappin' bitches up," and they haven't "been to jail for murder." One of the drug dealers insists that the "only niggas I hear representin' [hard-core rap] is 2pac, G-Rap and Wu-Tang."

That scene captures the bitter ironies and destructive contradictions that dogged the short, tragic life of Tupac Shakur. Tupac's hard-core image was sufficiently established to bleed through the frames of Lee's film--and through the high threshold for violence that gives too many young black males bottomless appetites for more thrilling, even erotic, displays of rhetorical, and yes, literal brutality. But that scene, like Tupac's conflicted career, also obscures truths that young black men must uncover in order to stem the tide of urban mayhem that they, to be sure, didn't create, but that they certainly extend.

After all, unlike the drug dealers in *Clockers* who sit around debating the merits of hard-core hip-hop, real black gangsters don't always scoop up a gaggle of gangsta rap tapes to ease them into the right frame of mind for mugging, mutilation or murder. Since they're already living the life, they often seek escape through music with decidedly uplifting themes, music sparked by edifying romantic and social ambitions. Notorious, real-life, gang-banging, "Monster" Sanyika Shakur, for instance, writes that he favored Al Green. And just think, all those wiseguys of yesteryear just loved Sinatra *flying them to the moon* and dropping them off in *New York, New York*, always doing it his way. That's a useful rejoinder to those who argue a strict one-to-one correlation between art and social anarchy.

But it's also a useful lesson to black kids about the limits of "The Real," and its relation to "The Represented." Like the drug-dealer in *Clockers* who lauds Shakur for representing the real hardcore in his raps, black kids, indeed, so much of black culture, is obsessed with racial and cultural authenticity. The obsession for authentic blackness, for "The Real," is driven in large part by the need to answer narrow, stereotypical, racist portrayals of black life. The gestures, nuances, contradictions, complexities and idiosyncrasies that define black life-- elements often ignored or steamrolled in homogenizing white views of black culture-- crowd the artistic visions of black writers, performers and intellectuals. Then too, such a quest often restricts the range of what is considered acceptable within black life-- "always put your best foot forward" is the unwritten rule governing many representations of black life. Ironically, the complexity of black culture is stifled under such a belief. "The Real" gets equated with "The Positive." What's considered negative in black life is determined by its unfavorable relation to an increasingly limited view of the authentically black. The negative in black life is viewed as the inevitable pathology that results from misdirection, confusion or concession to white stereotypes of black life. Such a view of black life is disabling. It alienates those whose lives coalesce at the outer perimeters of black respectability under which orthodox blackness masquerades. Those who depart from the positive ideal are stigmatized within black life. Such stigmatization evokes representations of black life that challenge the rigid orthodoxy of blackness, especially those visions of black culture that are viewed as bourgeois, high-fallutin', and hence, fake. The ironic quest for authentic blackness now comes full circle. It is wrested from the puritanical souls of the black bourgeoisie, only to rest in the hands-- and in the case of gangsta rappers, the throats-- of ghetto dwellers, redefined in the canon of new black authenticity as "Real Niggaz."

By now, though, the "Real Niggaz" who have established their own orthodoxy's, are trapped by their own contradictory couplings of authenticity and violence. Tupac's death is the most recent and perhaps the most painful evidence of that truth. For Tupac and a host of black youth, thuggery and thanatology have come almost exclusively to define the black ghetto. That's a sad retreat from a much more complex, compelling vision of black life that gangsta rap and hardcore hip-hop at its best helped outline. At the outset, gansta rap rudely and refreshingly resisted the artificial absorption of all black life into a narrative funnel of redemptive optimism or, at the very least, of reconstructive positivity. By thrusting the sharp edges of their lyrics into the inflated rhetoric of rigid black authenticity, they burst the psychic bubbles of blacks floating in comfortable, settled identities. Gangsta rap and hardcore hip-hop announced a ghetto renaissance: a flowering of vulgar self-expression rooted beneath the concrete predicates of polite discourse. But by joining verbal vigor to rage-- about material misery and racial hostility, about the avalanche of unheard suffering that suffocates black lives before they wake, walk or will their own survival-- hardcore rappers proved that theirs was a redemptive vulgarity. At their best, they showed that the real vulgarity was the absurd way too many black folk perish on the vine of fruitless promises, of neighborhood restoration, of racial rehabilitation. The hardcore hip-hopper proved that the real vulgarity was the vicious anonymity and punishing silence of poor black life, with which they broke faith every time they seized a mic to bring poetry to pain. Tupac knew this side of hardcore; explored it with a balance that can only be called "celeterrogation"-- the deft combination of celebration and interrogation. He rapped in his beautiful baritone about the plight of black welfare mothers. He skillfully narrated the thug's life as a cautionary tale of self-destruction.

But in the end, despite all of his considerable gifts, Tupac helped pioneer a more dangerous, even destructive, trend in hardcore hip-hop that, ironically, draws from the moral energy of the orthodox black culture from which he sought thuggish refuge. Shakur yearned to live the life he rapped about in his songs. That golden ideal was the motive behind gospel passions in black culture to close the gap between preaching and practice, between what one said and what one did. In the arc of Tupac's secular, gangsta ambitions, such an inversion of the gospel guide to black behavior proved fatal.

It would be simplistic to suggest that Tupac's death came solely from his own destructive desire to forsake "The Represented" for "The Real." After all, he was in part playing out the cards dealt to him, extending and experimenting with the script he was handed at birth, one written way before he came into existence. Some of his most brilliant raps are about those cards and that script-- poverty, ghetto life, the narrow choices of black men, the malevolent neglect of a racist society. But in falling prey to the temptation to *be* a gangster, Tupac lost his hold on the frustrating but powerful moral ambiguity that defines the rhetorical strategies and representational effectiveness for the gangsta rapper. In fleeing from art to the actual, from appearance to reality, from the studio to the streets, Tupac lost his life, and the most brilliant representations of the reality he confronted, and the powerful reality that his representations, like those of all great artists, helped to bring about. It is perhaps the greatest tragedy of a life cut short that Tupac didn't live long enough to trust his genius.

Eazy E, 2Pac, and The hip-hop Community: Have The Chickens Come Home To Roost?

by Craig A. Thompson

In late 1963, after the assassination of President John F. Kennedy, Malcolm X spoke at the Manhattan Center in New York. During his speech, he addressed the issue, "as you sow, so shall you reap." During the question and answer period, Malcolm declared that the shooting of Kennedy was a case of the "chickens coming home to roost." In other words, the violence perpetrated by the United States around the world had come back to haunt the U.S. in the form of an assassin's bullet. The tragic deaths of rappers Eazy E and Tupac Shakur should remind us of Malcolm's words, and force us to think deeply about the images that we project.

When I heard about the death of Tupac, I was driving to meet a friend. During the "shout out" period on the local radio station, many of the callers gave *big ups and shout outs* to Tupac, praying that he rest in peace. I immediately felt a tremendous sense of loss, because I knew of the impact that this brother had on our community. However, I also felt a tremendous sense of frustration, because the first picture that crossed my mind was the image of 'Pac standing barechested, proclaiming that he was living the "THUG LIFE." His violent death showed the world what living the thug life was all about.

When Eazy E died earlier this year, I thought about my last year of high school, when NWA came out with *Straight Outta Compton.* I recalled lyrics which glorified unprotected sex and promiscuity. I remembered listening to songs which told men that "a b---- is a b----," and encouraged brothers to "get theirs" with songs like "Easy Does It." His death from Acquired Immune Deficiency Syndrome (AIDS) showed the world what living this life would produce.

Our generation is at a crossroads. We have been presented with images ranging from players and queen bees, to thugs and female gangstas. Our response to those who have questioned these images has often been, "they are just images." We know that they are just songs and that these artists are not doing those things." Sometimes we said, "they are just reporting what goes on in our communities." We have never, however, collectively admitted that these images have done tremendous damage to our minds.

The so-called "hip-hop generation" has faced a great deal of scrutiny. The press has called this generation worthless and hopeless. Older people have dismissed this generation as misguided and lost. Politicians have unfairly blamed this generation for the many ills of society. Even members of this generation

(De La Soul, for example) have criticized the harsh reality that has been produced, claiming that "the stakes is high." The deaths of Eazy E and Tupac should serve as a clear and ringing alarm that tells us it is time to wake up!

If we continue to allow the images that we face to influence our spending habits, dress habits, speech habits and general actions, we may end up with fates similar to Eazy E and Tupac. Moreover, we will go down in history as the generation that killed each other from within. It is time for all people in our community who claim consciousness to begin "walking what we talk." We have to begin presenting images that promote strength without a gun, courage without an attitude, and beauty without half nudity. We must formulate a strategy for changing the way that we think, and construct a path that will lead us away from the twisted logic that tells us that getting A's in school is "white," and smoking Philly Blunts with your b---- makes you a "real nigga."

If we could hear voices from the grave, I strongly believe that both Eazy and 'Pac would tell us that they truly regret the actions which led to their untimely and undignified deaths. Both were in the prime of their lives, and lived for the roar of and love from the people who made them stars. Why would they want to lose all of that for sex or a trivial beef with someone? In the same vein, why would we want to lose the great potential we have to change this twisted world, for a *piece of a_ _* or a desire to *keep it real?* At this point, only heaven knows.

I pray that the souls of Tupac and Eazy E rest in peace. More importantly, I hope that their spirits remain with us, and guide us away from the paths that drove them from glory to the grave. If the chickens have in fact come home to roost, now is the time for us to gather them together, and keep them from getting away from us again.

epilogue: letter to my son

This letter was written the night of Tupac's death by Mutulu Shakur, a political prisoner locked down in the federal penitentiary in Florence, Colorado.

I love you whenever... forever. Tupac, so much I needed to say, so much you wanted to say. Many conversations between us within the ether, whenever... forever.

The pain inflicted that scarred your soul, but not your spirit, gave force to rebellion. Many couldn't see your dreams or understand your nightmares. How could they, Tupac? I knew your love and understood your passion. But you knew of your beginning and saw your end... racing toward it.

You taught and fought through your songs and deeds. RATT-TATT-TATT of words penetrating the contradiction of our existence.

Whenever... forever.

Who cares? We cared, Tupac. The Shakurs have been guided by struggle, prepared or not, whenever... forever. We've exposed our existence, naked from fear, to those who would hear the positive. Who would witness the stress, wear the tear of this lonely path. You couldn't have evaded the effect or the changes. You inherited it; it was in your genes.

But still, you danced your dance, you lived your life. You forced loyalty on those who would fake and shake at the true vision. You were Tupac.

Like the four seasons, we come to this planet taking form, becoming elements of nature. Some of us are only one season, and others like you were part of many seasons. This dynamic will scare most anyone who realized the burden at such an early stage of life. You fought well. We love you. We understand... forever, whenever.

Please give my love to our family. Ask them to help you on the other side. Tell Zayd, Lumumba, Abu, Brother Leggs, Mtaryi, Attallah, that they are to continue to help us down here. Shaker's love is strong. Whenever... forever.

Friday the 13th didn't mean a thing. Life is for living and dying, well. Whenever... forever. Allah knows best. We choose the quality of our life. We understand the pain of disappointment in the ones we love. You pushed so many away. Burnt so many bridges so they wouldn't follow you into battle against the demons you were facing. Knowing well to what lengths you would go, this battlefield of reality is littered with many meaningless casualties.

You never yelled out, "Somebody, save me!" You only asked for your soul to be free, whenever ... forever. You told us to keep our heads up, knowing the pain was coming. Knowing to look for the strength in the heavens. Set your soul free, Tupac Amaru.

Will your levitation be the awakening of us all-- the division unsettling to our dreams and goals, your passing demanding repentance and resistance?

We keep waiting, not in vain. We give you love. Give us love.

To my brother and son, these emotions are hell. I wish you well in the next journey. My soul aches for comfort. In our next life we will finish our unfinished journey. Whenever... forever.

For now, Tupac, we will hold our heads up. This journey is at an end, your ashes are in the wind. Friends and enemies will have to look to the stars. You are truly a star. A star navigating through the dynamics of this, your path chosen before you arrived. Lessons we've gained will materialize after you're gone. Whenever... forever.

Your family will keep the spirit high, for we are Shakurs. We are thankful for what life gives us. Through the pain and the struggle we are blessed by the victory. Go forward, Tupac.

The victories— we will teach your mission, we are thankful for you. We love you, Tupac Shakur. We ain't mad at you, we're better because of you.

So now I give you my tears so that I might assimilate your loss and I can live on in peace.

Knowing I will feed your spirit with my unconditional love, knowing you will need it on your next journey.

"Resistance" and "Thankful" ... one's name is the life's program for the bearer: Tupac Shakur. We will help them to understand your mission and journey. May Allah bless you for your deeds and forgive your errors.

Tupac come to me and give me strength.

Love always.
Your father, friend, comrade,

Mutulu

notes on contributors

Jenoyne Adams is a fiction writer and poet based in Los Angeles. A member of the World Stage Anansi Writers' Workshop, she is currently completing her first novel.

asha bandele is a 30-year-old writer living in Brooklyn, NY. Her first book of poetry, *Absence in the Palms of My Hands* was recently pubished.

Charlie R. Braxton is a poet, playwright and journalist form McComb, Mississippi. His works have appeared in numerous publications, including *Black American Literature Forum, The Black Nation, The Minnesota Review*, and the *San Fernando Poetry Journal*. His poetry also appears in *In The Tradition: An Anthology of Young Black Writers*. Mr. Braxton is the author of a volume of verse, *Ascension from the Ashes*, and the forthcoming *Reflections on Black Music: From Be-bop to Hip-Hop, and Ya Don't Stop*.

Marsha Mitchell-Bray is a product of LA's inner city, who did her undergraduate studies at UCLA, where she was the editor of *NOMMO*, the campus' African American Newsmagazine. Mitchell-Bray is a general assignment editor with the *Los Angeles Sentinel*. Bray is also the founder, publisher and editor-in-chief of a monthly multi-cultural youth newspaper called *Common Ground*. The popular paper has become an important voice for inner city teens, as many of the writers are high school students. She is also the author of *Women's Wedding Guide and Planner*. Bray enjoys spending quality time with her husband and their son, Malik.

Kenneth Carroll is the Washington coordinator of the WritersCorps programs, which conducts writing workshops in Washington, DC neighborhoods. He has written for a number of newspapers, including the *Washington Post, Washington City Paper* and *ONE Magazine*. His book, *So What! For the White Dude Who Said This Ain't Poetry*, will be published in December.

When **Jiton** writes from the spirits she loves being a novelist, freelance writer and editor. Her first novel *Sister, Mamma, Girlfriend*, will be published in the Spring of 1997. Jiton Davidson, 32, is a recent graduate of Morgan State University, with a B.A. in English, who plans to continue her education indefinitely. As the senior editor of *BAM*, an underground literary journal that she and a friend created while students, Jiton hoped to give voice to those young people who would remain silent-- for whatever reasons-- choking on knowledge that should be shared

Raoul Dennis an award-winning journalist and graphic designer. He is the former News/Politics and Technology Editor of *YSB* Magazine. A native of New York, and graduate of Hunter College, Raoul is the founder and editor of *GRIP*, a new cyberzine aimed at Black men.

Michael Eric Dyson, who in 1997 will become Visiting Distinguished Professor of African-American Studies at Columbia University, is the author of four books, including *Between God and Gangsta Rap: Bearing Witness to Black Culture*, and *Race Rules: Navigating The Color Line*.

Derrick I.M. Gilbert (aka D-Knowledge) is a Ph.D. candidate in Sociology at the University of California, Los Angeles. His essays have appeared in the *National Black Law Journal, Educational Policy*, and the *Encyclopedia of African-American Education*. As a poet, he has appeared in such films as *Higher Learning* and *Panther*, as well as on television shows like the *NAACP Image Awards, The Arsenio Hall Show*, and *The Apollo Comedy Hour*. He also recorded a poetry/spoken word CD, entitled *All That And A Bag Of Words*, on Quincy Jones' Qwest Records. He recently edited *Catch the Fire—A Cross-Generational Anthology of Contemporary African-American Poetry*, to be published in 1997.

dream hampton is a music critic and writer. The Detroit native has written extensively for *Essence, VIBE, The Source, Rap Pages* and *The Village Voice*.

Esther Iverem is the author of *The Time: Portrait of a Journey Home*, a critically acclaimed collection of poems and photographs published in 1994. Her poems and essays have also appeared in several anthologies, including *The Garden Thrives: Twentieth Century African American Poets*, edited by Clarence Major and *In The Tradition: An Anthology of Young Black Writers*. She writes about arts and culture for the *Washington Post* and has also written for *Essence, New York Newsday* and *The New York Times*. A native of Philadelphia, she is a graduate of the University of Southern California and received her master's degree in journalism from Columbia University. She lives in Washington, D.C. with her son, Mazi.

Bakari Kitwana is the Political Editor of *The Source: The Magazine of Hip-Hop Music, Culture, and Politics*, the former Editorial Director of Third World Press and the author of *The Rap on Gangsta Rap*. He is also a contributor to National Public Radio's *All Things Considered* and lectures on rap music and Black youth culture at colleges and universities across the country.

Toni Asante Lightfoot is a Washington, DC-based poet, who has performed her unique brand of "jazzoetry" across the United States and throughout the Carribean. She is the author of the chapbook, *Under the Neon Sky*. Her new collection of poety, *Kiss My Ear Like Jazz*, will be published along with her spoken word CD, in 1997.

Kierna Mayo is the Brooklyn-based writer and Special Events Editor of *City Limits* Magazine in New York City. Her work has appeared in *VIBE, The Source, Essence* and *Emerge*. She is a member of the Malcolm X Grassroots Movement, an organization founded, in part, by Mutulu Shakur, and dedicated to the promotion of self-determination among Afrikan people in the United States.

Tony Medina teaches English at Long Island University's Brooklyn campus and at Borough of Manhattan Community College, C.U.N.Y. He is the literature editor of *NOBO: A Journal of African American Dialogue*. The author of *No Noose Is Good Noose* and co-editor of *In Defense of Mumia*, his work is featured in the anthologies *In the Tradition; Aloud; Soulfires*, and *Spirit & Flame*, as well as many literary and popular culture publications.

Detroit native, **Jessica Care Moore**, 24, moved to New York City in 1995 to pursue her love for poetry. After making her mark on the open mic scene in NYC, she soon made history on the stage of Harlem's *It's Showtime At The Apollo*, winning five weeks in a row. The young poet is currently touring colleges and clubs in the US and Europe with her drummer Stix Bones. Moore currently lives in Brooklyn. Her poem, "The Words Don't Fit In My Mouth," is featured on Impulse recording artist, Antonio Hart's jazz album scheduled for release in February 1997.

Brooke Oden is a high school student in New Orleans. Her contribution to this book was originally written for her Creative Writing Class.

Mutulu Shakur is a doctor of acupuncture and a political prisoner currently held captive within the U.S. federal penitentiary system. He is a co-founder of the Black Acupuncture Advisory Association of North America, and a 30-year veteran of the struggle for justice for new Afrikans. In 1981, Mutulu Shakur was convicted of charges arising from the liberation of Assata Shakur and was sentenced to 60 years. He is the step-father of Tupac Shakur.

Craig A. Thompson, Esq. is a young lawyer from Baltimore, Maryland and President of Grand Vision Communications, an educational consulting firm. He lectures across the country to young audiences, stressing the importance of leadership, creativity and independent thinking. He is a contributing writer to the anthology, *Atonement: The Million Man March.*

AK. Toney is a poet, writer and performance artist. He is a member of the Anansi Writer's Workshop at the World Stage in Los Angeles. AK. is also a member of the Hittite Empire, an all African-American male performance art group, that has traveled across the nation since 1993. He is also a founder and member of a performance art group known as the Ibeji Players. AK. describes his poetry as, "urban vernacular slang that rides along the rhythms of hip-hop culture."

Omar Tyree is the author of three novels, *Flyy Girl, Capital City: The Chronicles of a D.C. Underworld,* and *BattleZone: The Struggle to Survive the American Institution.* He lives in Wilmington, Delaware.

this renaissance musician/producer/poet/performer/activist is taking art to another level. **wadud** births a hipnotically real sound that places the listener inside the music. he has performed at universities, colleges, and cafes throughtout the nation, as well as, europe. wadud's debut cd, *no additives or preservatives,* received rave reviews. he is currently completing his second album. "at a time when substantive music has settled at the bottom of society's glass, wadud comes as both a stir and a refreshing drink."

Angelo Antwone Williams is a native of Los Angeles, California currently pursuing graduate studies at the University of California at Davis. He is co-managing editor of *Clarion: The Academic and Arts Journal of African and African American Studies* at the University of California at Davis and co-managing editor of the literary journal *Crossroads: Divining the Word.* Williams also works as a disc jockey and commentator on an African-American community issues radio show in Northern California.

Derrick "Goldie" Williams is a poet and actor from Oakland, CA. Williams was featured in *Murder Was The Case,* the motion picture short produced by Death Row Records. He has also released a well-received EP, *Goldie The Poet*

Frank Williams (aka, P-frank) is a reporter at the *Los Angeles Times*. He is a graduate of San Diego State University and the Columbia University Graduate School of Journalism. His work has appeared in *The Source, VIBE,* and *Rap Pages.* The 25-year-old part-time poet and full-time black man is originally from Oakland, CA. His motto is taken from the Nas song: "Gun salute life rapidly, that's the ritual."

about the editors

Michael Datcher was born in 1967 on Chicago's Southside and raised on the Eastside of Long Beach, California. While a student at the University of California at Berkeley, he edited the national black men's poetry anthology *My Brothers Keeper*. After graduating from Berkeley in 1992, he started his masters in African American Literature at UCLA, finishing two years later. Datcher has written for the nation's top newspapers and magazines, including *VIBE, L.A. Times, Baltimore Sun* and *Buzz* and in 1993, he won the Walter White Award for Commentary. His essays have been anthologized in several books, including *TESTIMONY: Young African Americans on Self-Discovery and Black Identity* and the *SOULFIRES: Young Black Men on Love and Violence.*

In 1993, Datcher also began coordinating and hosting the critically acclaimed World Stage Anansi Writer's Workshop in LA's Crenshaw District, which attracts LA's top writers, as well as visiting luminaries like Sonia Sanchez and Komunyakaa. His first collection of poetry, *God Is A Black Woman*, will be published in February of 1997. He says, "I am a product of America's inner city blues, who has been educated on the verdant campuses of our nation's top universities. There is black beauty everywhere."

Kwame Alexander is the Founder, CEO, and Executive Editor of The Alexander Publishing Group [Imprints: BlackWords & Nandi Books], an independent press dedicated to providing publishing opportunities for young Black writers. He has edited three volumes of poetry: *Survival In Motion, Wake Up!* and *The Flow: New Black Poetry In Motion.* Alexander authored a recently published collection entitled, *Just Us: poems and counterpoems, 1986-1995.* The 28 year old poet/publisher has read and performed his work at over 50 colleges and universities throughout the United States & Europe, including Duke University, James Madison University, Howard University, Fisk University and The University of London. A graduate of Virginia Tech, where he studied under renowned poet Nikki Giovanni, Alexander is the proud father of Nandi Assata Alexander. He is currently completing his second book of poetry, *Kupenda: Blacklovepoems;* finishing a screenplay, and building the publishing house which made this book possible. *So It Is Written . . . So It Shall Be!*

*"Tell all my mourners
to mourn in red
'cause their ain't no sense
in my bein' dead"*

Langston Hughes

Tupac Shakur Discography

This Is An E.P. Release *(With Digital Undergound's Album, 1991)*
2Pacalypse Now *(1991)*
Strictly 4 My N.I.G.G.A.Z. *(1993)*
Above The Rim Soundtrack *(With Group "Thug Life," 1994)*
Me Against The World *(1995)*
All Eyez on Me *(1995)*
the don killuminati: the 7day theory *(Under alias "Makaveli," 1996)*
One Nation *(Forthcoming)*

Tupac Shakur Filmography

Juice *(1992)*
Poetic Justice *(1993)*
Above The Rim *(1994)*
GridLock *(1996)*
Gang Related *(1997)*

The Alexander Publishing Group is a young African-American owned house created to offer a widespread voice to the many gifted Black writers who have something to say, but are routinely passed over by other publishers. We publish commercial and literary fiction, non-fiction, poetry (under the imprint, BlackWords) and children's literature (under the imprint, Nandi Books) Please read our authors, continue to support us and we will continue to produce quality works by and about African Americans.

For more information on our company, or to share your thoughts, please write to us at:

Alexander Publishing Group
PO Box 21
Alexandria, VA 22313

notes